STUMBLING
BLOCKS

About Youth for Christ

Founded by American evangelist Billy Graham in 1946, Youth for Christ was set up to take the Good News relevantly to every young person in Britain, and over 65 years on it is still doing it. As a dynamic and cutting-edge youth work organization, workers serve local churches and go out onto the streets and into schools, prisons and communities as they pioneer new and meaningful methods of reaching young people with the Gospel.

God has used YFC to impact the lives of millions throughout Britain. The staff, trainees and volunteers currently reach over 250,000 young people every month. There are over 70 local YFC Centres, from the Isle of Wight to Inverclyde, as well as thousands of churches linked to the movement. Among other things, YFC invests in future evangelists and youth workers, provides outreach and discipleship resources for church-based youth work, offers residential opportunities and places a growing emphasis on peer-to-peer evangelism. British Youth for Christ is part of the wider international YFC family operating in over 120 nations worldwide.

For more information about Youth for Christ in Britain please visit www.yfc.co.uk

STUMBLING BLOCKS

Conquering the stuff that holds you back

Gavin and Anne Calver

MONARCH
BOOKS

Oxford, UK & Grand Rapids, Michigan, USA

Published by Monarch Books
an imprint of
Lion Hudson plc
Wilkinson House, Jordan Hill Road, Oxford OX2 8DR, England
Tel: +44 (0)1865 302750 Fax: +44 (0)1865 302757
Email: monarch@lionhudson.com
www.lionhudson.com

ISBN 978 0 85721 200 9 (print)
ISBN 978 0 85721 347 1 (Kindle)
ISBN 978 0 85721 348 8 (epub)

A catalogue record for this book is available from the British Library.

Printed and bound in the UK, June 2012, LH26.

To the late
Alex Buchanan,
who helped pray us both
over so many
of our stumbling blocks.

Contents

Foreword

I remember asking myself, "If following Jesus is all it's cracked up to be, why are some of my friends walking away from Him?"

They gave a whole bunch of reasons for not following Jesus any more: doubts, fears, boredom, personal crisis, unbelief, seeing a loved one suffer, anger, having better things to do with their lives. But I saw that even when it felt like the most sane thing to do, walking away was never as straightforward as they hoped it would be. One friend confessed, "It can be as difficult to walk away from Jesus as it is to stay with Him." I was heartbroken because he was walking away from the greatest love he will ever know. He was heartbroken too, knowing that he was leaving behind something or someone he would never be able to replace.

In my twenties I got wondering whether doubts and dark times will inevitably push us away from God. Is losing faith just a natural part of growing up for some of us? Do people who say "yes" to Jesus even against the odds have an extra dose of the faith gene that somehow makes it easier for them?

If you are in this place right now then this book is for you. You may have had Christians try to persuade you not to give up. You may even have experienced some of them wanting you to pretend that everything's OK or making you feel that you are wrong to be asking big questions about your faith.

The truth is that faith in Jesus is hard. It costs us everything, and Gavin and Anne know just how costly following Jesus really is. Rather than pushing them away from God, their willingness to say "yes" to Jesus, even when it hurt or felt like the craziest decision they had ever made, has changed them in ways they could never have predicted.

What I love most about Gavin and Anne is their integrity; their words ring true because they are writing about things they know all about. Although we might be tempted to see them as the kind of Christian leaders who've got it all sorted, they are courageous enough to let us in on the fact that their lives as followers of Jesus haven't been smooth or straightforward. Their honesty about their mistakes and vulnerability about their hurts is a powerful challenge to us to be real and open about what we're going through.

They are also full of love for friends, like you, whose experiences may be taking them to places they never thought they would go. If you're anything like me, in those early days or years of following Jesus you never made contingency plans for when things would get so tough that you would consider turning your back on God. And being in this place can be incredibly lonely.

But the whole point of this book is to remind you that you are not alone, and all your questions are worth raising and all your fears are worth facing. This book is not an invitation to just get on with it. It's not a slap on the wrist or a reminder of how "nice" Jesus is. It's a real, sometimes raw, always relevant, look at the stumbling blocks to faith we all face and an encouragement to do something about it.

You may have picked up this book having already decided in your mind to walk away from your Christian faith, in which case no book or talk or worship song is going to change that. Like the rich young ruler (Mark 10:17–27) you are free to say "yes" or "no" to Jesus – which is what makes Him so endlessly intriguing to me.

But if you are prepared to be real about your nagging questions, or feel ready to shine a light on why you feel so let down by God, or Christians, or both, then feel at home. You're among friends who care too much to let you just sit and wallow. I can hear Gavin's voice now at a youth event I heard him speak at recently:

> So you don't want to rely on the faith you had as a little kid? Good! You are sick of relying on your feelings to know whether God loves you or not? Good! You're dissatisfied with being spoon-fed Bible stories and know that from now on you really need to wrestle with the Scriptures for yourself? Good! Join the club!

As my friendship with Gavin and Anne has grown over the years, I have discovered how their relationship with Jesus literally rocks their world and changes theirs and other people's lives on a daily basis. Of course they have doubting days and difficult days. Of course they get stressed with small-mindedness dressed up as Christianity. Of course they get frustrated when church life speaks more about personal prejudice than God's reckless faith. But in following Jesus they have discovered life as the Author of life meant us to live and it's a life that they love in increasing measure.

May this be your experience too.

You belong in our family.

> That's how much you mean to me! That's how much I love you! I'd sell off the whole world to get you back, trade the creation just for you. So don't be afraid: I'm with you. (Isaiah 43:3–5, *The Message*)

Rachel Gardner
March 2012

Acknowledgments

Yes, the book is finished! To have got this far we know there are many people to thank who have brought this book into being. Particular thanks must go to Monarch, namely to Tony Collins, who keeps taking risks with our thoughts, listening to passionate ideas, and journeying with us to make them a written reality.

The core of this book was born out of the pain of a very difficult pregnancy and the story would not be penned now if it hadn't been for the incredible support of Kings Community Church in Brandhall – their constant practical help and faithful prayer, as well as their faith, brought us out the other side stronger than the way we went in. We are also overwhelmingly grateful for the tidal wave of prayer that came over from the United States – particularly from our family and friends at Walnut Hill Community Church in Connecticut. Together we know that this prayer support, coupled with all the prayer from churches and individuals across the UK, carried us through the most challenging time in our life so far. Thank you.

Our son Daniel would not be here now if it wasn't for the work of one man's hands: we will always feel indebted to Professor Mark Kilby at Birmingham Women's Hospital in, whose careful yet efficient work and faithful commitment to us as a family was God sent. For Mark and the Fetal Medicine team who assisted us and him, we are so thankful.

We thank God for helping us overcome this painful stumbling block, and so many others – without Him we would not know what it is to truly live. We want to thank those people whose stories of struggles have enabled this book to cover more than a Calver perspective – you know who you are!

For their sake all names have been changed in the following pages to protect their personal lives and walk with Jesus.

Most specifically we would like to thank our family and friends, particularly the Nott lads and lasses, Tim and Helen Dyke, Ruth Buttery, Jon Tattersall, Sarah and Mike Jordan and our 18+ group for helping us to work out, over, and through these stumbling blocks. Thank you for sticking with us. We love you all.

Gavin and Anne

Introduction

"A lot of people give up just before they're about to make it. You know, you never know when the next obstacle is going to be the last one."

Chuck Norris

Reality check

Turning thirty was a big deal for both of us. Realizing that not just our teens but our twenties were behind us was quite a shock. Gone was youth, faded into adulthood. A bit like starting a new year, these big milestones always cause us to stop and think about where life has taken us so far and the directions we want to take in the future. One of those thoughts was definitely about God and faith. Through it all, together, we have chosen to make living for Jesus the most important thing in our lives, and we carry the strongest of convictions that He is the only one worth living for – mainly because we believe that you can only truly live when you know the Author of life.

However, it has not always been a straightforward path. We have watched many of our peers make different choices, opting to live for other purposes or ideologies. We have observed friends journey with God and then give up on Him for various reasons. Seeing others give up on the faith that defines who and what we are has been particularly heartbreaking. At times it's been hard not to take some of it too personally, and we have had many conversations in which we have grappled with why stuff was happening and pondered over whether things would ever change.

We ourselves have been confronted with a whole host of challenges that had the potential to tear our faith apart. From struggles with church and Christians as teenagers to a real journey of pain in having children, there have been many moments when it has all just seemed too much to bear. However, in these times we have somehow managed to dust ourselves down, get up, and carry on. With the benefit of hindsight we are grateful for these difficulties, as they have given us more insight into why some folk just cannot reconcile following a God of love with their own personal circumstances.

We've called them "stumbling blocks": those things that trip us up and smack us in the face so hard that they cause us to give up on God completely, or stop us from even encountering Him in the first place. Each stumbling block is a separate problem that we have come into contact with, either personally or through knowing others who have struggled with it. At the centre of these pages is the stumbling block that caused us to write this book, because it is the one that has made us battle with faith, question God's fairness, and ask Him if He truly does love us. The one we are referring to is "When life is bad". Please forgive us for including such a personal chapter, but everything else you will read stems from it, as it awakened us to realize just how many things can stop us from committing to walking with God, or sap any faith we may have had.

Maybe you know what we mean. Perhaps you have faced some hideous pain in your life and you have no idea where God was in the middle of it. Or you dreamed a dream when you were younger but cannot for the life of you understand why a God of love hasn't answered your prayers. Maybe you relate to the person who says they had an experience of God years ago but He seems a million miles away from them now.

It could be that church has been the biggest struggle you have come up against in relation to encountering God – you just don't think there is any way you could belong in church – for you, it is a totally bizarre place to even consider going to.

Then there are the things that appear like a thief in the night and steal your faith away. You may not have seen them coming, you might not have realized until too late, but now when you look back you can say it was "that" that made you give up on God. Maybe you're a guy who cannot find a place in church or comprehend a "relationship" with God. Maybe you're a girl who knows there are no men to be found within the church walls, so you've chosen to live a different way. Perhaps you used to look up to someone "in the faith" but now they have walked away from it all and you are not sure you can continue; it's just rocked you to the core, and it seems as if there is no return. And then there are all those times you have prayed and prayed with longing in your heart for a particular outcome but it hasn't happened, or there just doesn't appear to be an answer; and then, faced with this reality, how can you possibly keep believing?

These are just some of the things that we have come across on our journey. There are many more. Worst of all, so often you cannot talk about these things until it's too late – well, not with Christians anyway – how on earth would they understand without judging you? So you've closed that chapter and moved on. Or you are trying to keep the pages open with hope but they are beginning to turn to a dull blur of distant conviction. Maybe, just maybe, you want to look into this Christian thing but there are so many questions – how can they possibly be overcome?

Being real

One of the most important qualities for us is honesty. We both grew up hearing "Just tell the truth" spoken time and time again by parents who meant well and who placed a massive value on honesty. At the time we did not understand why it was so important to speak honestly, but, after coming together with the same values and growing up a bit(!), we are convinced that truth is vital to healthy living. Telling each other the truth, speaking the truth to those we love – *and* those we don't know that well – is so important to us. I guess it's a core value in our lives. The more real we can be, the more we can expose some of the challenges we face, saying how we truly feel about them, then the more hope we have of establishing a faith that is real.

For a long time we have lived in a church where some things are clearly taboo subjects, where to doubt the existence of God or to question or give up on Him has been a total no-go area. Thankfully, with resources like Alpha we have begun to introduce the opportunity for people to say whatever they really feel and to question things they never felt able to raise before. Wouldn't it be great if we had a church that allowed those doubts and questions – those "stumbling blocks" – to be faced at *any* stage on the faith journey, so that they never grow into hurdles that cannot be overcome, so that the thoughts in our minds never consume us to such a point that we turn our backs on Jesus and walk another way? But, even more than that, we don't want the blocks to squash us to a point where there is no way through with God.

Only when we have talkeds about it have we found a way through: a way through the pain, a way through the unanswered prayer, a way of living with our frustrations in relation to church. Yes, talk to God first, but then talk to other people. Be real with one another and accept that walking with God brings challenges – but unless we are real about these challenges they will grow into an impassable barrier in our minds.

Faith finders

We cannot count the number of times we have heard about people who have given up on God or who have made a commitment to Him and then quickly turned away. We are also aware of many who claim that they cannot become a Christian because of their life circumstances or what it might mean for the rest of their life. We penned these pages because we want to encourage people to be real. We want to bring the stumbling blocks into the open, acknowledging that they exist and that they are potential show-stoppers in relation to faith.

But we also wrote this because not only do we want people to talk about issues like this, but we want the church to find a way of helping people through them, so that, whatever challenges they face, they do not have to go through life alone; they can know the Author of life through it all. Life is surely better when it isn't lived alone.

Maybe you are someone who relates to these early sentiments, but perhaps there is something in you that reads this and still wants to find a way of meeting God or of turning back and giving faith another go – of coming back to the Jesus who has never once given up on you.

Have a look at these stories and see if it's possible.

CHAPTER 1

Stumbling block:
Fallen idols

(ANNE)

"The fall from grace is steep and swift, and when you land, it does not make a sound, because you are alone."

Cari Williams (1995)

Homeward bound

It felt great to be back in the town I'd grown up in; to walk along streets that I knew like the back of my hand. Every now and then I'd look up and recognize a face from years past and feel that sense of belonging that only comes from an old home. I was heading for my old haunt, the Red Lion pub, to meet some friends whom I hadn't seen for years. I had chosen to walk because I wanted to soak up memories and enjoy being nostalgic for a while. It was fun to begin the evening like that, knowing that it would be followed by buzzing conversation that spoke the very stuff I'd been thinking: who was living where now? How many people had stayed living locally? Did "so and so" marry that guy she was with for years? It was exciting to wonder what the responses would be.

As I turned the corner and saw the pub in front of me, my excitement was suddenly tinged with nervousness. Even though I'd known the pub so well in the past and felt so much at ease within its four walls with my friends, it was different now. I hadn't been there for years and I hadn't seen some of my mates for a long time – I was different, they had changed, and the pub felt foreign.

Thankfully, although the decor was unfamiliar the faces weren't, and as soon as I saw my crew sitting in the same old area I quickly found my place among them. Warm hugs and bright smiles, along with a few sips of a pint, made me suddenly relax and the conversation began to flow as I had hoped it would. Yes, there had been a few marriages in the beautiful ancient Anglican church across the road; yes, a few folk had returned to the area – but many hadn't because they had met their partner in another part of the country. Anyway, it was far too expensive to live around here, and most of us had moved away for one reason or another.

The big difference for me was that I had found faith just before I had moved, and so most of my Christian life had been lived away from these old friends and this familiar setting. Most of them knew this to be true. They were aware that a lot of my views and decisions since then had been different from what they might have chosen; it made me slightly uneasy. At some point in the conversation my faith in God would come up – there was no way it could be ignored. Granted, they knew I had grown up in a Christian home, with my parents attending church, but they also knew the story of my teens, which definitely didn't resemble living my life for God. Back then it was all about booze, boys, and partying – to put it bluntly, it was all about me.

As everyone got comfortable and the drinks flowed, all kinds of stories were remembered. Faith naturally came up in the conversation, and of course I noted all the different reactions: some quickly turned their head to talk about something else;

others wandered off to the bar or the toilet until there were just a couple asking complicated questions and trying to throw me off my game. To be honest, I rather enjoyed chats like that – I knew there was no point trying to argue people into believing in God, it had to be their personal decision, and I had also learned that I didn't have all the answers. Even though I believed in God, it didn't mean that life was sorted and easy, but it had given me a sense of fulfilment that I didn't have before. As usual it was those who had drunk rather a lot more than the others who wanted to chat on; the rest were beginning to leave.

I was in no rush and happy to chat, so I stayed and listened. Eventually it was just me and the brother of a girl I had known well. At first I was pleased to catch up with him and felt glad to have the opportunity to ask how his sister was doing, but then, as he began to share, the atmosphere changed. He had been to church; he had been a Christian for a number of years, brought to Jesus through his sister, but after a number of difficult situations and some serious questioning he had decided that it was not for him. But instead of being accepting of others having faith, he was vociferous that it was all a waste of time. Never mind just turning his back on it, this guy wanted to argue me out of believing – he felt that all Christians had been brainwashed. He was as evangelistic about his humanist views as any individual I had ever come across.

Being quite sensitive and non-confrontational, I found his manner hard to bear and harder still to reason with. It felt like being smashed by a battering ram. I was finding it hard to gain space to breathe, let alone comment. Out came the incessant statements, worded as questions (though he didn't want answers; he just wanted to build his case): "Anne, how can you possibly believe in someone and something that you cannot see, especially when you don't always get answers? And then maybe you think you *do* get answers but surely you can put those down to 'circumstantial signs' [sarcastically]; surely you don't have any actual proof that there is a God out there speaking to *you*? How can you live for someone who lived so long ago and how the heck do you know that He is the right God to follow? I mean, do you honestly buy the fact that thousands of years ago someone died on a cross and it affects you today – right now? What a load of rubbish." The guy's scathing tone made me feel as if a post-modern Hitler was sentencing my Christian faith to death.

Although I felt beaten down by his comments and unable to respond, I didn't feel totally crushed. I was not defeated – not yet, anyway. I talked to him about my year out (at eighteen, when I had decided to give my life completely to God). I told him briefly how I had met God and *known* He was real. But after just a couple of sentences he tore my experience to shreds.

"You surely can't base your faith on experience, Anne; that is *so* subjective." By this point I felt as if I was standing in the dock trying to plead my case but quickly running out of time. I was going to be sentenced severely; my evidence was just not enough to keep me out of prison. I tried one last attempt.

"I know there is a God and I will go on believing in Him no matter what you say." I had given up making pithy responses and knew that I couldn't argue him into the kingdom – he was as hard as stone.

Then his final blow came, one I was not prepared for and one that left me, at the time, without a leg to stand on.

"Well, you know my sister is seriously doubting all this God stuff? You know, my sister who helped you meet Jesus and build the early stages of your faith? My sister, who helped you learn to speak in tongues and helped to lead on your gap year – yes, she is thinking it is all a waste of time now; she is coming to her senses. Oh, and the other leaders from your year out –

yes, some of them have stopped going to church; they have taken other paths to build success and do well in this world. After all, Anne, they know that they have to make the most of what they have before them, here and now."

As I left the pub my head hung low, lower than it had ever hung. His condemnation was clear: everything I had built my life on since I'd made the decision to follow Christ had been fake – I could not see it; I might have felt it, but that could surely be put down to circumstances, and some of the people who had told me it was real had decided it wasn't any more. So surely it was all over for me.

Instead of wandering back warmed by the joy of meeting old friends in my home town, and going over the memories in my mind, I was filled with fear and confusion. In all honesty I felt as if my faith had been drained out of me like liquid being sucked down a plughole. Yes, I had answers; yes, I had a response to what he had said, but what I couldn't handle was the fact that those people I had put my trust in, who had shown Jesus to me, who had played such a significant part in laying the foundations of my faith, had apparently turned their backs on God. Granted, I didn't know if that was really true, but, after being battered with all his thoughts and questions and then those final words, the blow seemed crippling.

What happened next?

I'd love to tell you that on my way home Jesus appeared to me in person so I could go back and prove His existence, but unfortunately that wasn't the case! In fact, looking back, I think what was about to unfold was far more important for my future. The weeks that followed were tough. I didn't turn my back on God, but I certainly questioned Him. I felt that there was an unsettled sea inside me – making me feel sick, nervous, and unsure. I didn't feel that I could talk to anyone from church but I talked to Gavin, I talked to my folks (who are Christians), and I talked to my brother, who was also struggling with faith. My mind was consumed with thoughts: I was so disappointed and upset – had these leaders *really* given up on God? I was desperate for Jesus to show Himself to me in a way that I could hit this guy over the head with. I wanted to prove my faith and shut him up so that he would never lead anyone to the dock in that manner again. Coupled with those feelings was doubt. Could I really carry on with this walk if I never "experienced" God in a powerful way again? What was I basing my faith on anyway?

I decided to go back to basics. After questioning others I realized that the only way I could calm the sea inside was to resolve it on my own. I watched some of the Alpha stuff again and found Nicky Gumbel's words immeasurably helpful. He had become a Christian through reading John's Gospel. I followed his example, opening the Bible and asking God to speak to me. I wanted to understand what had happened all those years ago and I wanted to know why I had decided it was true. As I read those words with an open heart and mind I remained sure that they were what I wanted to live my life believing. No, I didn't have an overwhelming experience of God, and, no, nothing really significant happened that would give me the ammunition to return to my friend at the pub, but, then again, would that really have been the best way? What happened instead was that I felt my anger towards him lessen and I actually began to feel sorry for him.

It was as if my faith had been torn into tiny pieces and I was there desperately trying to gather them together again and put them back into a picture that made sense to me. What was interesting was that when I stopped trying to solve it on my own and create my own picture, things started to slot together. My faith was not what it had been before. It was not built on the faith of others. It was not affected by the strong arguments and opinions of others. It was built on one simple thing. Because it had been taken apart, I had to find a seed that could make it grow again. That one simple seed was hope. Yes, I had decided that I believed what the Gospels were saying, but more than that I had come away from that evening at the Red Lion and reflected that I did not want to turn out like my friend's brother. I did not want to decide that there was no God. In no way did I want to live my life without God – after all, what kind of life was that? I mean, if life was just life then it was pretty depressing. There had to be more than this. To put it simply, I decided that I would rather live with hope in God than have no hope at all. From there the picture began to grow again and the brokenness brought a new strength that I had not known before.

Now, I know that none of this is straightforward, but the fact remains that, whatever happens, we are all still left with a choice, and I knew that I wanted to choose God. More recently I had a chat with a friend who doesn't believe in God, and she was telling me about her sister, who is still broken-hearted after splitting from her boyfriend over a year ago. Her sister had talked her ear off and wept all night over this guy and my friend said she felt that she had nothing left to say. She had sat and listened but ultimately she was just thinking, "You are going to have to find a way through this." For me that is where the rubber hits the road; there has to be more to offer than just a listening ear. Surely there is a God we can pray to who loves us and who will carry us through situations like this?

Keep going

It is especially challenging when those we look up to give up on Jesus. I can think of so many who have walked away from God for all manner of reasons: they had prayed for the healing of someone who then died; they ran off with a woman younger than their wife; life dealt them some blows and they could no longer cope; they had hidden their sexual orientation and this later came back to haunt them. In many ways the list is endless. For some people it isn't so much a fallen human idol as perhaps Jesus who has become the fallen figure in their minds – He died, after all! And then they become the fallen figures to us. They give up on God, stumble, and fall, but the broken pieces spread as far as us.

The challenge to us, then, is how much we allow those painful shards to dig into our souls. Can we keep going even if they do not?

Whenever Gav hears about another leader "falling from grace", he really struggles. I rarely see Gav negatively affected by other people – he is one of the most positive characters I know – but when someone to whom he has looked up as a leader suddenly falls, it instantly causes his head to hang low, especially when the "fall" appears to be a self-centred hedonistic crusade that damages everyone and everything around the person concerned. When this happens, and when leaders disappoint us, we have to shake ourselves and work at taking our eyes off the fallen hero on the floor and look up at the King of the world, whose grace we keep walking in.

At these times our faith has to find a way to stand on its own two feet and not just be influenced by others. Just because someone we know and love falls from their pedestal and maybe loses their faith, it doesn't mean we have to as well. Anyhow, who else is going to show them Christ's love through it all?

Indeed, it must have been hard even for the disciples as they saw within their group one betray Jesus, another deny Him, and yet another doubt Him. Christians around us will make mistakes and will tragically turn away from God. We must pray that this doesn't lead to our turning away too.

While not being swayed ourselves, we should also pray that those who do turn away will soon come back – and, more than that, give them the space to do so. In the Old Testament, when King David famously had an affair with the soldier Uriah's wife, Bathsheba, he audaciously sent Uriah to the front line in battle, effectively murdering him (2 Samuel 11). Here was David in an absolute mess, a fallen idol if ever there was one. However, the story doesn't end with his fall. Theologian Michael Eaton puts it this way: "Everything David did he did in a big way. He was guilty of big sin. But then his repentance was equally great. His restoration started at the point where he was convicted of the sinfulness of what he had done and frankly confessed it."[1] If people confess and walk through repentance, genuinely hungry for God again, we have to allow them to get up – otherwise what is true grace all about? The truth is that we believe in a God who can melt the hardest of hearts and bring them back to Himself. He could do that for you right now.

Hope

If Christ lives in us by the power of His Holy Spirit (Colossians 1:27), then we have a hope that is worth living for. Whatever hits us, whoever else drops away, and however hard life might be, there is something greater at work in us and through us to sustain us. This is the hope that I cling to – hope that, no matter what people throw at us and what they try to convince us of, we are not shaken. It's that old verse that makes complete sense in this context: "Now faith is being sure of what we hope for and certain of what we do not see" (Hebrews 11:1). Literally – if everything is challenged, what decision will we make? If even those who have been our greatest influences towards Jesus give up on Him, will we still stand strong?

I was putting my five-year-old daughter to bed the other evening and, as always, I prayed. Halfway through the prayer I opened my eyes and saw that her eyes were open and she was distracted by one of her teddies.

I stopped praying and said, "Amelie, do you want to talk to Jesus with me?"

Her answer (not easy to respond to at that time of night!) was, "Well, Mummy, I'm not sure. I can't see Him."

I thought for a moment and then said, "Yes, I know we can't see Him, Amelie, but He is always with us and will take care of us."

She frowned and responded, "But what's the point in talking to God when we can't see Him?" A pause. "Anyway, the angels take care of me; why do we need God?"

Talk about stumped – I was at a loss for words!

The thing is, it is all about faith, isn't it? And explaining faith to a five-year-old is challenging. Our society demands that we see and prove everything, otherwise what is the point in it? My friend in the pub was essentially saying the same: "Let's build a world and a life based on what we know is a concrete reality, not on what we believe. The unseen is a waste of time."

I responded to my daughter by reminding her about space: "The planets are up there but most of the time you can't see them when you look up – you just know they are there; you can't see God either, but we believe that He is watching over us." (I struggled to find anything more literal to say!)

The reality is that we lose something massive if we stop believing in things that are "unseen" – particularly if we lose faith in a God who created us and has a hand in each one of our lives.

Surely having hope in God gives a sense of purpose to lives that would otherwise have little meaning? Surely having hope in God gives us freedom, because we grasp who we are and what we were designed for? And surely a God who loves us so much that He would send His Son to die for us affirms us to such a point that we then learn how to feel love and share that love with others? Leaders will lose their faith; people we respect will not journey on with God. Will we let them influence our faith, or are we going to build it on a different basis? Will fallen idols create a stumbling block that causes another casualty – as they almost did with me – or is there a way through?

The bottom line is this. If you died tomorrow you would lose nothing if you believe that there is more to life than this. However, if you die without faith, you could find yourself without anything. I don't know about you, but we would rather go on believing.

To think about...

- What is/was your faith built on? Is/was it something that could fall apart? Perhaps other people have laid the foundations of your faith, but Jesus wants it to begin with you and Him.

- Do you feel let down and disappointed by others, so much so that the hope has gone? Is it time to find hope in God again?

CHAPTER 2

Stumbling block:
Faith stealers

(GAVIN)

"There is no such thing as a good
influence. Because to influence a person
is to give him one's own soul. He does not
think his natural thoughts, or burn with
his natural passions. His virtues are not real
to him. His sins, if there are such things
as sins, are borrowed. He becomes an echo
of someone else's music, an actor of a part
that has not been written for him."

Oscar Wilde[1]

Sunday-school ban

Fair enough, I was never what you might call one of the "angels" at Sunday school, but I was hardly an imp of Satan either. My best friend, Paul, and I were often up to mischief as young lads, and it would frequently land us in trouble. For some reason we did our best to disrupt whatever was being organized at church and, although never deliberately malicious or rude, we were most definitely cheeky.

I remember one Sunday morning particularly clearly because it was so different from the rest and so damaging that it has remained in my mind ever since. Paul and I arrived at church to find the other young people in our group sitting in a circle chatting with one another. Instead of including us in the circle, no one turned to look at us. We were greeted with hostility. Granted, we were a little late, but this was over the top.

One of the leaders turned to us and, without even getting up from the circle, waved us away with her hand. She told us in no uncertain terms to go back to where we'd come from, as we weren't welcome there. We were now officially banned from attending for six months. There was some garbled justification to do with thinking about our actions, but by this point we'd closed our ears to anything that our Sunday-school teacher had to say. We were just fourteen years old.

This was not just a six-month ban from Sunday school that passed quickly and was soon forgotten; it was so much more than that: it made me furious with church. I clearly remember turning to Paul and saying, with as much meaning and authority as I could muster, "I hate church!" I simply couldn't believe that we'd been rejected. I knew the Bible quite well and couldn't understand how a group that allegedly followed the example of the Son of God, who "hung out" with tax collectors, lepers, and prostitutes, could take so violently against two young minor rogues. Yes, we could be trouble, but in this case we'd done nothing worse than turn up a few minutes later than the rest.

Over the next four and a half years, I did not take a step into church unless it was Christmas or some other occasion that I couldn't avoid. My childlike faith was battered and my hostility towards Christianity grew. One of the saddest things about it was that the youth leader had absolutely no idea how her actions had affected my feelings and decisions about the church.

It is no exaggeration to say that, like a thief stealing things away in the darkest hour of the night, that leader had come and taken my faith at one of my most vulnerable moments. And when I woke in the light of the next day my life was strewn with questions and fury in relation to God. So often people do things quickly and without much thought, but they can affect our faith dramatically and leave a horrible mess behind.

If I'd had the benefit of hindsight and maturity I would have realized that we need to accept that other people can rob us of our faith through their actions, conduct, and words, and therefore I would have been more alert and perhaps less affected. Unfortunately, I was not an adult and I did not have that level of awareness, which makes me even more certain that we have to watch our actions and be aware of how damaging they can be to young Christians.

Expectation

Many would say that growing up in the church is a real privilege: it provides a guaranteed time to hang out with your friends every week, a safe place to learn about life and God, and a sense of community. But there is another side, isn't there? There is definitely a real struggle for young people growing up in church and one of the biggest challenges they face is the level of expectation laid on them, to behave a certain way, to be a certain someone. Some of these expectations may exist only in our minds, but we feel them anyway and they can damage or destroy our faith.

When Molly was little she was a beautiful girl with large round eyes, always dancing around in her ballet shoes and pretty floral dresses. She was this pure young girl whom everyone loved and cared for. But when Molly got older, things changed. As a teenager she looked and smelled different and the reaction towards her at church shifted. In her teens

STUMBLING
BLOCKS

Molly wore dresses that were more like belts and make-up that changed her whole appearance. Every Sunday her lips were deep red and her eyes so dark you could hardly recognize her. Molly had more piercings than you could count on two hands, and her golden hair was now black as night. She was not the approachable person she had been, partly because of her new look but also because of the lanky lads who would sometimes accompany her through the church doors. One glare from one of Molly's men and the congregation would immediately look away. After feeling so relaxed with Molly as a little girl, the majority of adults now struggled to know where she was "at" and therefore gave up even trying to approach her to begin a conversation.

At sixteen Molly fell pregnant. It wasn't planned, and she was heartbroken. The one place she would have sought solace as a child would most definitely have been among her "family" at church, but things had changed now. Molly knew they already frowned on her appearance and on her boyfriends – what on earth would their faces look like if she showed up with the baby bump she had been trying to hide? Molly felt lost and alone, but she decided to leave her church. She just could not face returning to those people and seeing their expressions. And if following God meant surrounding yourself with people like that, she was out. Church, in Molly's mind, was somewhere you could only go if you "fitted in" and followed the rules. She assumed that she was no longer welcome. The weight of the expectation that she should look and behave a certain way was so great that she turned her back on Jesus. That was it – that was all it took for Molly's faith to be "game over".

It was a bit like that with Barry too. Barry battled for years with his sexuality and couldn't face "coming out" because he believed that if he said he was gay the church would shun him for ever. Church was the one place he felt he belonged, and he didn't want to lose his family. For some reason Barry thought that he had to get himself into a state of being strong enough to tell the church that he was gay, and then he would have to leave. In his brain it felt like a nasty secret that he was ashamed to speak of, but he knew he had to at some point, in order to be honest with himself and with everyone around him. It was like a need to go to confession but with no forgiveness there to be received.

When Barry finally made the decision to "come out" he did not wait for a response from the church – which he presumed would be total judgment; instead, he automatically lost his faith and gave up coming to church. Instead of expecting any measure of grace, Barry assumed that the worst would happen and he would be thrown out because he was different. In his mind he could not be gay and a Christian. In Molly's mind she could not be pregnant and a Christian. They both lost their faith in God because of this perspective. The weight of expectation had stolen their faith away, and they would never return.

What kind of church is this?

Being treated terribly, living under heavy expectations, and dealing with challenging people can be the sort of stumbling blocks that we find impossible to overcome. Some of this stuff causes a fury to rise inside us. What sort of church are we part of? Is it really a church that stops people finding a way through these messes – that stops individuals being real about who they are and what they are facing?

Research by the Barna Group shows that "one-sixth of young Christians (17 per cent) say that they have made mistakes and feel judged in church because of them".[2] Now don't hear us wrong. If we choose to follow Christ, we do try to live differently because we want to have the best kind of life we can, but that doesn't mean we don't make mistakes. Getting things wrong or stumbling is part of human nature, and – especially through those crucial years of growing up – we have to be able to fall and get back up again. How can it be possible for a young lad to feel that because his orientation is gay, he would automatically be thrown out of church? Yes, the church would encourage him not to live an actively gay lifestyle, but surely their open arms of love should be wider than any found outside? Surely their acceptance should be as Christ's would be – unending?

We have to be able to humour people over their fashion choices – not sending out a message of "You are not welcome here" because they look different. I once read a sign that said "Do not loiter, skate or play by these steps under any circumstances" and I was absolutely appalled because the notice was sited by the steps leading up to the church doors. What young person in their right mind would want to go near that church building after reading a sign like that? Even before they step through the doors they feel unwelcome and judged for doing normal teenage things! No wonder Molly felt that she had to leave when she got pregnant if such minor things as "loitering" are viewed so negatively.

We have to expect people to blow it. There cannot be a 100-per-cent success rate for good behaviour at church, because we are all human. We place such a massive expectation on people, but what is the message we are sending? Do we give the impression of writing people off?

At a Youth for Christ residential camp, two fourteen-year-old lads came up to me to chat about the evening before. They had both encountered Jesus for the first time that night and were so passionate; the first one exploded with "I f***ing love Jesus, Gav!" followed by the other one announcing, "Too right, I f***ing love Jesus too!" As you can imagine, I was quite taken aback by their words, but at that moment they were merely using an expression that they deemed appropriate. In six months' time you might hope that their choice of language would be different, but in that moment of enthusiasm and glimmering new faith, the last thing I should have done was react to what they had said. Those of us who have been Christians for a while need to be careful about how we deal with these initial stages of discipleship and not pass judgment or make unhelpful comments too quickly or forcefully.

There is such a challenge to the church to handle things more lovingly. Rather than passing judgment, we should offer an arm of grace. The Bible is littered with examples of God not giving up on His children and always welcoming them with open arms when they have messed up. We need to consider how we are behaving towards people in the church. How would Jesus handle them? He loved first. He did challenge people not to keep sinning – but He loved them to the point at which they realized that there was a "better" way to live, where their pain could be less and their baggage less destructive. He wants us to have that life because He loves us and wants the best for us, not because He wants to judge us. We know that the life the prodigal son can have with his father will be so much better than the life he has had out on his own.

But are we offering a welcome like the one you would find in the father's house?

Healing, *pleeeaaassseee*

Another issue that can bring an end to our spiritual journey is unanswered prayer.

We clearly remember praying and praying for Julie, longing that God would reach down with His mighty hand and heal her of the vicious cancer that raged through her body. We had seen and known God heal before and we longed for Him to do the same for Julie. After all, she loved Jesus so much and had lived for Him for years. Why was nothing changing? Julie had treatment after treatment. She lost her beautiful thick raven-black hair and lived with her new patchy head, becoming weaker and weaker, and thinner and thinner, and struggling to look after her three small children.

Julie's husband was a wreck. He could not understand how we could be praying and praying, petitioning God to do something on his wife's behalf, and yet there was no change in her situation. It gradually became clear that Julie was going to die – it was just a matter of time. With help from friends with the children, a hastily packed suitcase, and some desperate prayers, the couple headed off to a healing conference for a last attempt to "get Julie healed".

It was not to be. This precious lady was not going to live, and, no matter how much praying and longing went on, Julie grew steadily worse. She battled with God. She felt angry, then bitter, then upset, and finally – at the very end – peaceful. The cancer had taken hold in such a way that it took her whole life, and the only "nice" thing that happened was that when she left this world she had all her close family around her.

This was totally devastating for her three small children and for her husband, Glen. Glen could not grasp how her life could be taken from her in such a hideous way, how this loving woman, whom he knew Jesus loved, was not "allowed" to watch her children grow up and develop into the fine adults they would become. How could a so-called "loving God" let this happen to his family? Glen wrestled for ages with this pain and with bereavement and struggled to manage the kids without his wife. Now it was his turn to feel angry, bitter, and devastated.

And again, just like the thief in the night, in the darkest hour Glen's faith was stolen away.

"If there truly was a God, there is no way this stuff would happen in the world," he concluded. So often we can cry out to God for something to change and, when it doesn't go the way we hoped and longed for, we can end up (for a whole host of reasons) turning our backs on God.

Room for questioning

Surely there has to be not only a hand of grace, but also space to process thoughts and feelings. Many of us seem to sit on messy life issues or moments of doubt and never find a way to work through them before it is too late. It is as if the anger, resentment, or frustration is eventually allowed to take away our faith – the one thing that can sustain us through all life's challenges! And yet there is a stigma associated with talking about how we really feel. Maybe the church is somehow afraid of honesty and vulnerability because it might reveal how fragile we really are. The truth is that if Glen had been able to talk and battle through his emotions, wrestling openly with church friends and with God, he might well be in a different place today.

It is strange to think how contradictory this behaviour is to what we see in the Psalms. David, the shepherd boy who eventually became king of Israel, always found a way to share his deepest pain and struggles but still keep his faith. David's greatest highs and lows are recorded in the Psalms and yet no one questions his relationship with God. In one of the psalms he says, "Be merciful to me, O Lord, for I am in distress; my eyes grow weak with sorrow, my soul and my body with grief" (Psalm 31:9). David finds a way not to blame God but to cry out from his gut for help. He doesn't hold back from sharing everything he feels, and one could argue that he had a stronger understanding of God because he worked through his wobbles.

If Glen had been able to keep talking, keep finding a shoulder to cry on, keep experiencing support from the church; if he had felt OK about pouring his heart and soul out to God time and time again – even in his fury – there's a possibility that losing his wife would not have been the stumbling block that knocked him down for good.

What next?

There has to be a way for the cheeky teenage chappie, the pregnant girl, the hurting husband, and the guy struggling with his sexual orientation to feel that they can make mistakes and battle with God, yet still be loved. They surely have to be able to be themselves and be accepted. That doesn't mean that the church should become wishy-washy about what it stands for, but that we should never be the reason why a person's faith is stolen away. Wouldn't it be amazing if we encouraged a new culture where people didn't blame God for the world's mistakes but rather found a way to share from the heart, like David, with one another and with God? Then ultimately there would be more of us in church, able to hold on to our faith and support one another, as knowing God really is the one thing that will never let us down.

To think about...

- Have you been badly hurt by the expectations of people in the church? Remember that although people or circumstances might try to steal your faith, you can always be real with Jesus.

- Maybe you feel that you are beyond the love of God because of who you are or what you have done. Try sharing your circumstances with someone you trust. It won't be as bad as you think and Jesus would never write you off.

- It's time to pray that as Christians we might handle the broken better and provide space for people to share what they are really facing.

CHAPTER 3

Stumbling block:
I feel sceptical and cynical

(GAVIN)

"Generally I don't like doing remakes, but I think that's more in the cynical world of Hollywood where normally remakes are purely for commercial reasons."

Gerard Butler, actor

The Healer

When I was growing up as a teenage lad in south-east London, America felt like a distant land that I only read about or saw images of on the TV screen. I never imagined going there – to me it was just one of those huge places on the other side of the world where people spoke strangely! However, over fifteen years on, I cannot believe how familiar the self-proclaimed "land of the free" has become. I never dreamed that I would visit my parents while they were living in Chicago, Baltimore, and currently Connecticut, and over the last fifteen years I feel that the culture of America is one I have in many ways got to grips with. Indeed, today I love the USA, and have many friends and family members there. However, this was not always the case. Let me take you back to 1996 and an initial impression from my youth that was profoundly unhelpful.

My dad, who had always been incredibly strong and hard-working, was taken ill – he was so sick that he was advised to take a year off work. It was a massive surprise to those who knew him, as he was always the one who could keep going no matter what. It was strange to suddenly have my dad around when he had been away so often, and it drove my mum mad having him under her feet when she was so used to her independence! As Dad slowly recovered, he got itchy feet and was desperate to get out. It was the year of my GCSEs (high-school exams at sixteen), and once I could get the inconvenience of those out of the way I had an unbelievably long summer off. These weeks of boredom on both our parts led us to plan a holiday in America – just the two of us.

All our previous holidays had been under canvas in northern Europe, so the idea of going to the other side of the world at sixteen years old, with my dad, was incredibly exciting. I was somewhat overwhelmed when I arrived. Everything was massive, people ate so much, the drinks were refilled before we had even finished them, the language was more different than I could have imagined, and all the architecture was so much newer and more, well, artificial than I was used to. I was clearly half the world away from home. The shopping malls needed their own postcodes, the people at least appeared friendly, and I was falling in love with the American dream. It really felt like the trip of a lifetime. Here I was, far away from the hassles of normal life and all the nonsense at home – not least about church.

At that age I couldn't have been less interested in church. At that point in my life it just didn't make sense to me. There was a constant battle between me and my folks about the need to go in the first place. With my dad being a man of the cloth, one of the few drawbacks of the American trip was the fact that I had to go to church over there. We pulled up at a church building – though it looked nothing like what I had expected. This place looked more like a shopping centre than a house of prayer. It was massive, with a huge illuminated cross and grand signage proclaiming its name. I was taken aback by the grandiose nature of it all, what with being from a poor part of London where dilapidated church buildings were often now used as carpet warehouses or, at best, were still hosting Sunday worship but looking decidedly tired. Never before had I seen such a monstrosity of a church.

We walked in through the gigantic doors having our hands shaken incessantly and being told time and again that it was so wonderful to see us and we must make sure that we had a nice day. Was it really that great to see me, and did they actually care what my day would be like? As I stepped in I had a really good look around and couldn't believe what I saw. The entrance hall alone seemed to go on for ever, with its rolling walls and carpet. There were endless corridors leading off into opaque surroundings with a million little rooms off them. As we wandered down one such corridor there were people scattered everywhere – some on their own, others huddled in noisy groups, but the common theme was coffee cups. We wandered past a clear "no-go" area, which I immediately felt drawn towards (probably precisely *because* it was prohibited!). I quickly noticed a man loitering a short distance away, clearly hoping to engage me in conversation, so I turned on my heel and scuttled after my dad.

As I went along I began to notice that there was an obvious fashion rule for the place: floral dresses for women and white suits for men. My skater trainers, jeans, and T-shirt made me feel uncomfortable, as I was suddenly not invisible and anonymous. The smell down the corridor was instantly recognizable from my usual nights out at home – fake tan. (Doesn't it stink of feet?!) Everywhere I looked, people appeared caked in tan mousse and looking as if they had just stepped out of a photo shoot for a home-delivery clothing catalogue. We joined the catwalk taking an escalator (an *escalator* in church, when most of the world's population doesn't even have clean water!) up to the first floor and into the auditorium. It was incredible – much grander than any theatre I had ever been to. I gazed around, taking in all I could see.

Eventually the show – I mean service – began. I had never seen a church with a stage towering ten feet in the air! The mega-green curtains at the sides gave a theatrical feel and the stadium-like seating arrangement did nothing but amplify the sense that this was a production. Some popcorn would have made me feel right at home. It would not have surprised me if an old lady had started coming round halfway through, offering small tubs of ice cream.

The service started with the choir belting out songs – their perma-smiles fixed in place and rows of immaculate white teeth glistening in the glare of the lights. The entire choir looked as if they had been teleported in from some beautiful island. Did this church not have any ugly people? I had found the only place in America where no one was overweight!

The place roared with life as the singing became livelier and livelier. A couple of songs were repeated over and over, and the whole crowd whipped themselves up into a real frenzy.

When they had finally finished their "set", the pastor made his grand entrance. The crowd went wild as their leader and hero entered the arena. He was small in stature and seemed unimpressive, but to his home crowd he clearly had a direct line to Jesus. He led the crowd in a few enthusiastic "Hallelujahs" and the action intensified.

"It's time for Jesus to set some of you free from illness right now, so have the faith and come to the stage for prayer."

Person after person was brought into the action and the pastor kept declaring over each one, "With faith you are set free and healed." The more of this that took place, the more frenzied the crowd became. It felt like the most surreal form of "entertainment" I had ever encountered. As I sat back and observed the behaviour I was a little perplexed about why people with such physical ailments were being made to climb the stairs onto a ten-foot-high stage. Why on earth were they not being treated with a little more subtlety? Despite my teenage cynicism, I wanted to ask why this was such a crass show, and not a sensitive moving of the Spirit.

The band had begun by playing quietly and slowly, but now the music was getting louder and more intoxicating. Suddenly the noise of the drums intensified and it became all too clear that the action was moving to a crescendo. As the crowd waited with bated breath to see what was going to happen, a man on crutches and in a full body brace was helped onto the stage by two stewards. This was clearly going to be the crowning moment of the service – obviously God was going to set this man free for all to see. You could feel the excitement and anticipation in every part of the auditorium as people pressed forward to catch a glimpse of the action. The atmosphere was so intense that I thought some of the people standing at the front were about to pass out!

As I peered more closely at the man on crutches being helped across the stage, I suddenly felt physically sick to the pit of my stomach. I studied him for a few seconds more and knew without a doubt that I had seen this guy in the "no-go" area earlier. It was the very same man who had been walking around freely before the service. He had been strolling about without a care in the world in the same blue shirt and cream chinos that he was now wearing under his newly acquired body brace. I have been blessed with a photographic memory and there was just no doubt in my mind – I had seen this guy walking around less than an hour before. I was in total shock and my stomach was profoundly queasy. I could almost feel my blood boil as this show of fabrication and dishonesty continued in front of my eyes.

I could hardly watch what followed. The pastor came over and interviewed the guy. He said he had been in a car crash five years previously and since then had struggled greatly physically – apparently there was nothing the medical experts could do for him now. The pastor proclaimed to his tribe that there was only one solution for this, and that was the healing power of Jesus. The arena erupted in screams of joy and delight, and cries of "Help him, Jesus". Clearly no one had a clue that this was all a fraud.

As the pastor laid his hands on the guy's head and prayed that in the name of Jesus the man would be set free from his physical iniquities, the sick feeling within me intensified. How could this be happening? The prayer was passionate, the crowd even more so, and they gazed on in amazement as the guy got out of his body brace and dropped the crutches and moved around freely – even dancing on the stage. The atmosphere in the auditorium was one of shock and awe as the crowd celebrated what could only be a miracle of the highest order straight from heaven. It was a faith-filled atmosphere of delight.

I felt absolutely furious. How could people be deceived like this? It was simply a piece of human fabrication and manipulation, and I knew it.

After the service I had a go at my dad about it. "How could they do that, Dad?" He too was shocked to the core. "Why would any Christian ever need to be so manipulative, forceful, and insecure?" I could not understand how they could follow a Jesus who said,

All authority in heaven and on earth has been given to me. Therefore go and make disciples of all nations, baptising them in the name of the Father and of the Son and of the Holy Spirit, and teaching them to obey everything I have commanded you. And surely I am with you always, to the very end of the age."

(Matthew 28:18–20)

If Jesus has that authority and people follow Him and He gives us His power, why on earth would there be the need to fabricate anything? And I wasn't even saved at that point!

Personal experience

I just wish that the story above was an isolated incident. Sadly, that is not the case. Growing up in a charismatic (lively) church, there was never a shortage of crazy things going on. There was a time when I was younger when the church became preoccupied with people being prayed for and falling over or making animal noises and other such bizarre things. Many referred to it as a time of blessing, though to me as a teenager it seemed like a freak show. The church would have receiving meetings and at these all manner of things would take place. My real problem with it all was that it seemed like a perennial Christian bless-up with very few positive outcomes. Why would God be doing this without any noticeable change in people's lives? Where was the fruit from it all? It seemed that folks were living on a quick-buzz form of faith that was achieving nothing.

Things really came to a head for me when I was being prayed for at one such meeting. I was not really interested in being prayed for, but the nature of the meetings would whip everyone up into a great frenzy which created an intoxicating whirlwind of atmosphere and passion into which I had been dragged. So I found myself in the queue, waiting to be blessed. After breathing over many others and seeing them fall over like dominoes, the preacher man finally found his way to me.

He prayed with great passion over me as if my very salvation depended on it. I have to say I was starting to enjoy it all. The atmosphere was buzzing and I could feel adrenalin pumping through my veins. Here I was on an emotional high that required no pill! However, I was not falling over and was certainly not growling like a lion. The preacher was not to be defeated and so placed a hand in the small of my back and attempted to push me over "manually".

I was furious. What on earth did he think he was doing? If God wanted me to fall over when prayed for then why did this mere mortal need to push me over? Why did I have to fall over anyway? All of a sudden I felt that I was seeing this entire meeting in a different light. This wasn't God doing something dramatic; it was people fabricating something to hype a crowd. Why? For what purpose? I had heard about Jesus doing miracles and all kinds of things to help, bless, and equip, but not for entertainment or a legal high. I looked the preacher directly in the face and snapped, "If God is real then He doesn't need you to do this for Him." I then stormed out of the meeting.

The critical eye

How was I ever supposed to become part of a church whose current members behaved so oddly, who were willing to twist truth and force things that were not real? And, more than that, how was I supposed to believe in and follow a God who needed humans to behave in such fake ways? For a long time my sceptical and cynical stance grew and I became deeply negative towards and wary of people who said that God had done something dramatic in their life. I did not want to associate myself with a church that didn't believe that God could move by Himself. If *they* didn't believe in Him, how could I?

The problem with scepticism is that once it takes root it is tough to shift, and you fall into the habit of criticizing everything. Even now there are moments when I question things that allegedly happen "in the Spirit" – not because I don't believe God has the power to do whatever He chooses, but because I'm not sure of the motivation behind the manifestations. Many of my friends have rejected Jesus because of just this kind of behaviour. Some Christians make it so hard for younger people to follow Jesus. If they would just let God do His natural and authentic thing then there would be no problem!

Sadly I am also too aware of the insecurity of so many Christian leaders. The temptation is there for them to force and manipulate things in order to feel better about themselves. You see this profoundly with altar calls. No one responds first time around, so the preacher keeps having a go until people do. In the end the preacher feels good but no one is really sure what they have responded to.

If God is all-powerful, all-present and all-knowing, then perhaps Christians should trust Him a little more and be satisfied with His outcomes, however stunning they may or may not be.

Hypocrites?

The problem with Christians behaving as described above is that it opens the church up to clear accusations of hypocrisy. In my own experience, nothing seems to push people further away from the church than the hypocritical behaviour of those within it. According to research published in *USA Today*, 72 per cent of Americans feel that the church is full of hypocrites.[1]

These figures would be at least as high in the UK, and probably even higher. We really need to make sure that we are not directly contradicting our message with our behaviour.

Often it is said that we should "practise what we preach", but I wonder what the local vicar would say this coming Sunday if, instead, he "preached what he practised?" Would his ministry be over? Would it actually be more engaging? This is all conjecture, but I do believe that greater effort needs to be made to present a consistent message.

However, despite all these inconsistencies, they do not equate to all Christians being hypocrites. As with so many areas in life, a vocal minority makes it hard for the rest. We also need to take a second look at what a hypocrite actually is. The theologian R. C. Sproul puts it as follows:

> The charge that the church is full of hypocrites is manifestly false. A hypocrite is someone who does things he claims he does not do. Outside observers of the Christian church see people who profess to be Christians and observe that they sin. Since they see sin in the lives of Christians, they rush to the judgment that therefore these people are hypocrites. If a person claims to be without sin and then demonstrates sin, surely that person is a hypocrite. But for a Christian simply to demonstrate that he is a sinner does not convict him of hypocrisy.[2]

We are all works in progress, and as such have a long way to go. It seems that the calling that God is putting on our lives is to find a way to be true to who we really are. Not to put ourselves on a pedestal, from which we can only fall, and not to pretend things are more "godly" than they actually are. Whatever role we have and whatever life we are living, we all remain sinners in need of a Saviour. If this truth continues to permeate us and we are not trying to promote anything we are not, then the power of Christ can really shine through. Then we will truly be blown away by what we see, because we know it has to be God.

Moving on

With a deeper spiritual maturity than I had in the days of the American evangelist and other church experiences, I have learned to see that the problem I had was not with God – He is all-powerful and can do what He likes; it was with people, and to some extent it still is. Why they would feel that they need to manufacture the presence and power of God is beyond me! But now I can see how deeply insecure they must be and how manipulative, and how scared they are to really put their faith in Christ. I am also increasingly aware of just how many people feel the need to do things *for* God rather than let Him do His work His way, using us as the tool in His hand. We struggle not to take control for ourselves. Sadly, many can lose faith if they have been stung by so-called "miraculous" moments, or by people proclaiming something and then acting totally differently away from the stage.

But we can trust a God who may choose to do things differently. Would you have really chosen the disciples? Would you have first appeared after the resurrection to an outcast like Mary Magdalene? Would you have spent only three out of thirty-three years in active ministry? God's ways are not our ways, and Lord help anyone who tries to manipulate things on His behalf. One day they will have to explain to Him why.

We must not allow others to stop us in our journey with God. Their actions should never be the stumbling block that knocks us over. With time I have realized that my negative experiences are the exception, not the rule. They represent how a tiny minority of followers of Jesus might choose to behave. American Christianity has so many positives and I mustn't allow one negative experience to tarnish this. I have seen how powerfully God is at work in His American church family since that day and know it was a far from representative experience. British charismatic Christianity is vibrant, and again the conduct of one leader, in one situation, years ago, cannot be allowed to diminish this or take away from all that Jesus has done in people's hearts and lives over those years.

Other people's faith and their subsequent behaviour should not serve as the marker for whether we stick with Jesus. They sadly played a part in my adolescent attitudes, but I'm just pleased it wasn't the final chapter in my walk with Jesus.

To think about...

- Have you seen things done in the name of Jesus that you know are not from God?

- Don't let the acts of others convince you that Jesus is not real. We are all sinners in need of a Saviour; we all get it wrong sometimes. The insecurity of many leads to a need to sometimes "push" things seemingly on behalf of God. However, when God is at work there is lasting fruit.

CHAPTER 4

Stumbling block:
When the feelings go

(ANNE)

"Much to learn, you still have."

Yoda, in *Star Wars Episode II: Attack of the Clones*[1]

The big event

I remember, as a teenage girl, taking my place on the hard carpet with my friends, crossing our legs and folding our hands in our laps, like some sort of protective mechanism against the world around us. We piled our jumpers in the middle – no doubt because we had observed other groups of friends do the same – and then, instead of nattering as we usually did, we paused and looked around. There was a different atmosphere in the venue tonight. The hundreds of other young people sitting on every side of us were also quieter than usual; there wasn't the normal banter from the stage, and I couldn't help noticing that the worship leader was getting ready to sing much earlier than he had before. I felt a rather strange sense of peace descend on me, almost as if I was the only person in the room, with no distractions – not, as in reality, sitting in a huge warehouse-like building with hundreds of sweaty bodies my own age.

An announcement came from the front: "Good evening, everyone. It is great to see you all again; can you believe it is the third night already?! This evening we have decided to scrap the normal games section and move straight into worshipping God with the band. We prayed as a team and really feel that God wants to meet with us and us with Him, and we are excited to be a part of what He might want to do."

There was a murmur of approval from the floor and we all slowly began to relax. The crossed-legs, arms-folded approach was seen less and less across the room, replaced with open hands and hearts. The venue leader began to pray, the worship band began to sing, and then en masse we rose to worship God.

Something incredible happened as we sang together. There was not only that amazing sense of peace, but I felt so alive and excited as I began to declare who Jesus was and is. Looking around me I could see that many others were affected in the same way. Some were crying, others smiling, yet more kneeling – each one worshipping God alone, yet together. We seemed to feel the tangible presence of God, and He was pleased with the praises of His people. I felt I never wanted it to end.

What confused me was how to connect what was going on outside in the "real world" with what was happening here in this place. It was quite obvious to me that God was real and worth following, but whenever I left such a situation and the feelings returned to "normal" it was very difficult to go on believing, let alone go on living for Jesus.

As an example, even before heading to the youth venue that night I had felt cross with my folks for not letting me stay out as late as the on-site curfew, and frustrated with my friend because she was clearly getting more male attention than I was. I had had some conversations about some people that would have been better left unspoken – yes, because they were gossip, but also because of my choice of language. And this was among my Christian mates! I knew it wasn't great, but in my brain that was who I was and that was how I fitted in with the rest of the group.

Home didn't bear thinking about – that was a much bigger can of worms. What on earth would they think if they could see me now? Although I was standing in this venue with my heart crying out to God, and definitely experiencing His power and greatness, I just found it impossible to acknowledge Him at home. How could I be part of the popular crowd if I had faith in God? How could I hang out with my friends and be accepted if I chose to live a different way? And to be honest I wanted to be part of that world and I wanted to have fun, and I could not work out how the two could hang together.

So deep down I knew that when I went home this faith stuff would crumble rapidly once again, and would not be pieced together until I returned to the festival the following year. And although, yes, I would make unhelpful life choices when I returned home, sometimes I did have all the right intentions and I did want to live life for God. But there was one thing that always made it impossible: the feelings disappeared. All those moments in the venues worshipping God – all those experiences of sensing God and seeing Him at work and perhaps becoming familiar with His presence – they were gone as quickly as my friends could say "Welcome home!" or even earlier, when I went back to my accommodation.

What I found hard and enviable at times was the experience of my closest mate. He went to church and believed in God and somehow seemed to be able to be a Christian and yet also find a comfortable place in a group of friends. On our return from the festivals he would agree with me that the feelings often evaporated, but it didn't stop him from following God. I have to say that it took me until my late teens to accept that if I was going to choose to live for God, it would not necessarily mean feeling constant highs or a sense of His presence all the time.

We cannot live by feelings

Even now, when we watch God at work in young people and see the mountain-top experiences happening in front of us, we are concerned about what happens when they go home. It's partly because we know they are human like us, but also because we know we cannot live off the feelings for months on end. Also, there is no hiding from the reality that life is a mixture of mountain tops and valleys, with everything else in between. There is no avoiding the bumps in the road, and the mountain-top moments can never be considered normal. We always hope and pray that the experiences they have at the festivals will be more of an equipping for the world outside, rather than just a "God-bless-me" moment that will fade away.

It is so tough nowadays to find a faith in God that is not dependent on feelings, especially for a young person. We live in the kind of society that is always looking for that next "buzz" or for something that will satisfy the needs within us. Whether that is alcohol, sport, games consoles, Facebook, or Twitter – we are always doing things that give instant satisfaction. The danger is that God becomes just another item on that list. So we go to Him, as we did to the festivals year after year, have the experience, enjoy it, and then move on. Jesus becomes one of those "quick fixes" to get us through the month or even the year – a spiritual shot in the arm to make us feel better for an instant.

Now we are obviously not in any way against festivals. In fact, we spend most of our summers being blown away by all that Jesus does at them. They provide an incredible place for Christians to come together and for people to find faith, but we must be careful not to sell the lie that those feelings last for ever or that they are the basis for our faith. Jesus never preached a gospel that said, "Come and experience Me through quick fixes"; it was "Come and follow Me with everything". It was sacrificial, it was costly, and it meant their whole life. However, that doesn't imply that it was a boring, sad life.

It might seem at first glance as if we are suggesting that when the feelings go, living for God is not only tough, but it is tedious as well. But we *can* live life to the full following the greatest world-changer who ever lived – day in, day out, even without constant warm, fuzzy feelings – with a growing knowledge of Him and a desire to love Him and His people. Instead of looking for a quick fix to satisfy ourselves, the gospel message flips that on its head and says, "Look for ways to love others with the love that I have given you" – that sense of blessing others is a far more incredible and lasting feeling than the "bless-me" approach we sometimes buy into.

Faith instead of feeling

How many times have we heard the line "But I can't feel Him; how do I know He is there?", or, even more commonly, "I just wish He would let me know He is real"? It is definitely something we have been guilty of thinking. "Please God, just touch us and then we will be OK." Our humanness seems to have begun to dictate whether we can have a faith that lasts. Countless times we have told each other and those who'll listen that living for God is about Him, not about us, and that we don't really deserve anything from Him.

Our faith since our late teens has not been built on mountain-top experiences (because we are now well aware that there are not many of them and they don't last long), but is founded on a hope of someone greater than us who holds us even when we can't feel it, and lifts us even when our humanness stops us being aware of Him. It is a lasting relationship with Jesus, implying that the honeymoon period has to end and the fuzzy feelings get replaced by a solid foundation of belief that there is a God of the universe who cares about every one of us. Truth is not dependent on how we may feel on any given day. Truth remains the same, and in the words of Jesus, "Then you will know the truth, and the truth will set you free" (John 8:32).

This means we should always have hope. Hope for the future and for today, hope for next year and for eternity, hope in the Saviour of the world. This hope is a wonderful thing. As a quote from Gav's favourite film says, "Hope is a good thing, maybe the best of things, and no good thing ever dies."[2] When the feelings go and the encounter with God that seemed so vivid is little more than a hazy memory, we must cling to the hope we found in Jesus. The feelings may evaporate quickly but the hope never dies!

Everything seems instant

So many of our relationships break down – how many of us have parents who have not been able to stay together, or have known them have more than one life partner? Tragically, marriage rates in England and Wales are at their lowest since records began, with 2009 seeing the lowest number of marriages registered in any year since 1895.[3] Commitment to all things is on the wane, not least commitment to another human being "till death us do part". There is an old saying that, when it comes to making breakfast, the chicken's involved but the pig's committed! How many of us are prepared to commit ourselves to anything any more?

Often we find ourselves walking in and out of relationships simply because the feelings seem to fade or we just feel that we don't love that person any more. But real love surely means working at it and through any obstacles ahead. Love can't be reduced to an instant emotion that requires no perseverance. Sometimes it brings pain that is so immense and destructive that feelings are numbed and decisions uncertain or deeply complicated. And whenever there is a difficult, damaged relationship and we cannot work out why it's gone wrong, how do we find a way to trust someone again, let alone trust God?

It is very challenging to communicate the truth of a God who will not break our trust and who will stick by us when the first years have passed or when we mess up. It is quite hard to persuade someone that Jesus loves them so much that even when they cannot feel Him He is still with them and will never leave or forsake them. We need to find a way to convey the fact that a relationship with Jesus is immeasurably more amazing than even the best ones we have in our lives already, because His love is not based on feelings; it is an unconditional love. We must not allow the many fragile human relationships to cloud our understanding of who God is. He is far more than any other could ever be. In the words of the psalmist, "a father to the fatherless, a defender of widows, is God in his holy dwelling" (Psalm 68:5).

Yet as well as being so far above us in all ways, God does actually care about our feelings. Jesus definitely wanted us to experience His love and grow in His power so that others might know Him – otherwise why would He bother sending the Holy Spirit (John 16:5–16)? Jesus sent the Spirit as counsellor, to convict us of our sin and guide us into all truth. As we read in Acts, this was without doubt an experience of our powerful God, as they saw tongues of fire separating and coming to rest on them and then were filled with the Holy Spirit and began to speak in other tongues as He enabled them (Acts 2:1–4). So receiving the Spirit is clearly an important thing for a Christian, and often comes with some sort of experience of God. How incredible is that?

A "bless-you" approach

God continues to fill us with His Holy Spirit today and that was definitely my experience in those youth venues as a teenager. The danger comes when we find that our faith is limited to those experiences and that, when the feelings disappear, there is little left. We also encounter problems when we only want to follow God when it is like the mountain-top moment. It just can't always be like that. The reality is that the Spirit of God is still at work in our lives, but that doesn't mean we remain as "consumers", constantly craving a new "fix" of His power; rather, we should be getting up and doing something with what we have gratefully received. It's interesting that the first thing Peter does after receiving the Holy Spirit is stand up, address the crowd, and explain to them what has happened and how they can meet Jesus. At the end of his talk we read, "Those who accepted his message were baptised and about three thousand were added to their number that day" (Acts 2:41). Peter does not just sit about waiting to see if he can get more of the "fix", or waiting for the feelings to fade; he gets up and tells people about the truth that he has found. Challenging!

God wants us to find a faith like that, a faith that cannot be shaken. Instead of thinking we cannot feel Him any more, we turn our attention to how we can grow in Him and then know more of His power at work in our lives through the Holy Spirit. We need to think less of ourselves and more of others; instead of God blessing us, we bless God. Ironically, in doing that we will end up feeling blessed too!

What is needed is a generation who go beyond fragile feelings and persevere and stick with Jesus for the rest of their days. Admittedly, this is very hard in the "instant" society that we live in. When I was growing up, the television repair shop at the end of the road did a roaring trade. Yet twenty years later you wouldn't dream of mending a TV; you would just throw it away. When I was younger, if the zip went on a pair of trousers it would be replaced. Now you would throw the trousers away. We live in a society where everything is instant and disposable. We must work hard not to allow culture to influence us so far that our faith mirrors society and becomes instant too. Faith must be a journey of perseverance and commitment.

Instead of viewing feelings as a sort of self-help tool, it is much more effective to see them as something that equips us to go into the world ready to live for Christ. At one of the summer festivals last year, there was a moment when we watched all the young people in one of the venues raise their hands in the air, worshipping Jesus, and then bow their heads in prayer and adoration. As the song ended, Gavin and I smiled at each other as we recognized the presence of God being sensed tangibly across the venue. Then I looked out over them all again and imagined every single one of them armed for battle and ready to be sent home. It was as if their worship and their experience of God had poured strength into each one of them, uniting them and equipping them with the full armour of God to go out and take on the world.

Now, as adults, we wish we had been able to picture feelings like this, rather than wondering when they would subside and then questioning whether God was real. We wish we had been able then to use our experience as a fuel to help us to live for God wherever we were going, and to keep asking Him to fill us to overflowing with His Spirit even if we couldn't feel it happening. The truth is that we can trust that the Lord Jesus will do it anyway, because He loves us more than we can ever ask or imagine.

To think about...

- Do you wait for the feelings in order to be sure that God is with you? Perhaps He wants to increase your faith no matter how you feel right now.

- Hang on in there even when you feel empty, dry and alone. The truth is that He never leaves us, even if we feel as though He has.

- Base your faith on what is true – not on how it feels.

- It is so challenging to try and live for Jesus surrounded by people who don't believe in Him. It doesn't matter how committed you are to Christ – it is tough! Pray for strength every day.

CHAPTER 5

Stumbling block:
I hate church

(GAVIN)

> **"I'm having the best day of my life, and I owe it all to not going to church!"**
>
> Homer Simpson

Have you ever watched that programme where the parents go away for a week and the kids are left to turn the family home into whatever they wish? It's an absolutely crazy idea: who in their right mind does that? Some people, obviously. You sit and watch the poor returning parents looking totally horrified as they observe their once beautifully decorated lounge with its chocolate-brown leather suite transformed into a windowless cinema with tiered stadium seating, their spacious kitchen with all mod cons replaced with a bleak burger bar, the children's rooms transformed into a karaoke bar and mega ball pool, and their antique four-poster bed swapped for four individual sleeping pods so the whole family can sleep in the same place. The look of utter desperation on their faces makes you want to laugh and cry in equal measure: laugh because they were nuts enough to agree to it, and cry because you know how devastated you would feel if it happened to you.

The thinking behind the programme made me wonder what might happen if the established church decided to go away for a week, allowing those newer to this Christianity thing to reform the church into what they wanted it to be. Can you picture what might happen? Would it be as disastrous as the programme? To us it feels strangely exciting, but there are probably many churchgoers who would be terrified by such a suggestion. The more we think about it, the more aware we become of how different the church can be from the rest of society. How the hopes and desires of those fresher to the church are often very different from those of the older attendees, and as a sad result they can feel like outsiders in the one place they should call home. It's arresting to consider how great a divide exists between the church and society. This divide can prove to be a real stumbling block to those on their early journey with Jesus. How sad it is that the Bride of Christ itself can in fact be the thing that pushes people away!

Take the timings of just about every UK church's main Sunday services. These can be a real obstacle to attendance for many, with changes in work patterns, long-standing previous commitments, and a multitude of other time pressures. Yet these timings in and of themselves are surely not that important! In fact, they have more to do with milking cows than with Jesus – but how many of us are busy milking cows this century? Not many! You would milk cows at 9 a.m. and 5 p.m. This would take half an hour, followed by half an hour to get clean and a further half an hour to get to church. When we meet for a Sunday service we are still being dictated to by this activity! In the mornings it must be at 10:30 a.m. (or 11 a.m. if you want to be slightly different) and in the evenings it absolutely has to be 6:30 p.m. We make these timings inflexible and sacred, and place the most value of all on the need for people to be at the morning service. Are service times really that important and inflexible, or have we just become caught up in tradition? Do they "fit" with the world that we live in right now? What might Jesus say about all this?

And then consider the service itself. Do we need to be singing love songs to Jesus (as if He were our girl- or boyfriend) led by a guitarist at the front, followed by a talk that's far too long, dull, and disengaging, and finishing with an awkward time of stilted conversation as we all drink horrible coffee from polystyrene cups? Was this really what Jesus meant when He said that He would build His church (Matthew 16:18)?

Now there are some from outside the established Christian community who would sit quietly in church, accept the way it is, and not want to upset the status quo. But the reality is that the majority of newcomers, if they had the choice or the opportunity, would probably do things differently. Therefore, because things often don't change, there comes a stage for a large percentage of new followers (adolescents in particular) at which church becomes an incredibly difficult concept, and many will say that they can't connect with it, or, worse still, they simply declare, "I hate church."

This is painfully pertinent to young people. Why does it happen? We personally believe that there are a number of reasons (to explore this area in greater detail, please see Gavin's first book, *Disappointed with Jesus? Why Do So Many Young People Give Up on God?*, Monarch, 2010). First, there is suddenly an increased desire for independence. Adolescents might seek to break away from church as they begin to make their own personal choices. Second, the adolescent can often feel ignored in church. This is probably because many older believers honestly struggle to communicate with today's young people. The truth is, though, that if we don't, who will? Third, adolescents can claim to hate church because they feel as if they have no place there. All three reasons can have dramatic consequences, but we believe the overarching challenge is how to make young people feel that they belong.

Children are different. They are easier because they haven't reached the stage of independence, they are not ready to question, and in the main they are happy to go along and play with their friends. They are not at an age where they have influence – they still go out at the back of the church to their activities and don't affect the style of service. Adolescents, however, fit into a different bracket, and their capacity for causing problems is far greater. They often want to do things differently. They have stylistic preferences that can upset the equilibrium. In some local churches, an organ always leads the worship, but many of the youngsters want drums if not decks. Although DJ-led rapping might be a bridge too far, even the idea of using a data projector is too much for some. Perversely, it often seems that the young people are expected to compromise far more than the older ones. After all, it's been their church for fifty years... The question is, do they still want it to exist in twenty?

Karl Barth is often quoted as saying that Christians "should hold the Bible in one hand and the newspaper in the other". It is hard to find definite references for this, and the closest on record is from *Time* Magazine: "[Barth] recalls that 40 years ago he advised young theologians 'to take your Bible and take your newspaper, and read both. But interpret newspapers from your Bible.'"[1] Whatever his exact words, the principles certainly still apply, though the newspaper might today be replaced by an iPad. Indeed, the ministry that we're involved in, Youth for Christ, operated for many years under the mission statement "Geared to the times, anchored to the Rock". Yet is the church ever really like this? Does it really ever appear to engage its truth with the sociological framework that it is part of? If we fail to engage with society, how will we ever be anything other than a stumbling block to those outside our walls?

The one thing about Christianity that above all else should

never change is the substance of the message. This can be summed up by the most famous Bible passage of them all, John 3:16–17:

> For God so loved the world that he gave his one and only Son, that whoever believes in him shall not perish but have eternal life. For God did not send his Son into the world to condemn the world, but to save the world through him.

The truth of this never changes; it is eternal. The Christian message is fundamentally simple and there is no need to complicate it. Some attribute the following quote to St John Chrysostom and others to John Calvin. Either way, its truth is powerful: "The Son of God became the son of man so that the sons and daughters of men might become the sons and daughters of God."

Again, this truth never changes. The problem that so many Christians seem to have is that they mix up substance and style. The substance of the message never changes yet the style should change like the wind. Whatever it takes to communicate the truth behind the universe should be used. The style is totally changeable; it's the substance we shouldn't tinker with.

The history of the church contains a plethora of examples of people taking the truth of the word and applying it to a new environment. This was made even more apparent by the nineteenth-century pioneer James Hudson Taylor. He was an English missionary to China, who went on to found the China Inland Mission and was known for embracing facets of Chinese culture (such as dress) in a way that previous missionaries had chosen to ignore. Here was an evangelist who didn't stand out unnecessarily and make Christianity look inaccessible, but instead fitted in with cultural norms in order to gain a platform for his message of hope. We should surely seek to emulate his example more wholeheartedly within our own cultural vacuum.

An inclusive family?

Picture the scene of a dad taking his two pre-school children to the video shop to rent a film for the three of them to watch. Dad may desperately want to watch *Rocky* or *Rambo* but his four-year-old daughter and three-year-old son are instead waving madly towards the *Dumbo* box. What is he to do, when their preferences are in such stark contrast to one another? Common sense dictates in the end, and Dad must face the reality that the next couple of hours will see him settling down to watch the Disney classic with his kids. When it comes to family life the number-one priority is for everyone to be involved in inclusive times, and so the choice of what to do or watch will always reflect the needs of the least mature. This applies beyond young people to other groups within the church who might also otherwise be left out.

Why then do all the rules change when it comes to church life? Why on earth do we expect less mature individuals to integrate fully into our existing way of doing church without being prepared to be more adaptable? Bearing in mind the fact that the more mature Christians do need teaching and nurturing, they should nevertheless make every effort to integrate with the newer ones. The spiritually mature should be more willing to sacrifice their own preferences, and not just expect the less mature to do so. It's time we started seeing church as a true family and reflecting this in all we do. Maybe this is unrealistic, but I honestly believe that if some of the older folk compromised just a little, and met others in the middle, then the future of the church would look a great deal brighter. We mustn't keep claiming to be a family if we don't behave like one.

Whether we like it or not, young people in particular are going to struggle within the confines of the church. As teenagers they are going to want to break out and discover new things for themselves. The problem is not in the struggle, but in how the church chooses to respond. We need to create an environment that is youth-friendly, so that even when young people kick against a wall we still welcome them in with open arms. This can be achieved in all kinds of ways, from inviting them to have a say in church meetings, and playing sport together, to just having a conversation over coffee (or perhaps hot chocolate would be more age-appropriate!).

When young people say, "I hate church", too often the church's actions seem to say, "Well, we hate young people!" Anne and I love young people and we love the church, and we long to see the two brought together. As people who are attempting to stand in the gap, we plead with you to join us in making church a place where adolescents can feel welcome. Let's create an environment that can live up to the mandate of being the Bride of Christ, where young people are loved, empowered, and blessed. If this is happening in the church and, by association, the home, then adolescents will feel part of the community and respond positively.

A little while ago, I left Anne and the kiddies in bed and headed up north to preach. After the talk I had the privilege of meeting four wonderful ladies (all in their nineties) who were desperate to see the young people of their town reached for Jesus. They felt they had nothing to offer but wanted so much for the church to have a future. I talked with them about the great needs of young people and encouraged them to try to reach out. They bravely set up a youth group for those aged eleven to fourteen, arranging to meet once a week. Six months later I was thrilled to receive a letter from one of the ladies saying that there were now thirty young people coming to their group on a Thursday evening. As these ladies prove, it doesn't matter how old you are; anyone can bridge that gap. It just takes a heart of compassion for young people and a desire to see the church have a future.

Let's create a new programme for the church: one where the adults might go away and be missed. One where the young people wouldn't want to change anything radically and the adults wouldn't be too scared to return. One where new Christians find a welcoming and inclusive environment. One where all people are working, loving, and serving so well together that the number of lost souls being saved is doubling every week. One where no one gives up on Jesus. That's the church we dream of.

What style might work?

It's always easier to criticize than to defend, so, with a desire to be constructive, we wanted to look at what type of church might work in today's society and across the generations. The post-modern theologian Leonard Sweet suggests in one of his books[2] and numerous articles[3] that anything that works in today's society and culture is...

Experiential
Participatory
Image-driven
Connected

Therefore, if the church is going to connect with post-moderns, we have to become more EPIC. But what does it mean to be EPIC in respect of style? Let's take a look at IKEA.

I remember very well the IKEA store opening up in Purley (just outside south London), near where I grew up. To a young teenager, the place was amazing when compared to any other furniture shop. After all, what could be more boring in essence than a furniture shop? But IKEA was something else altogether. It was so *experiential*. In place of the usual shop floor was a path that led you on a journey around the place. The whole thing became an experience in itself. You weren't shopping; you were on a journey.

It was *participatory* in that you were involved and could try new things. If you wanted to buy a chair then not only could you sit on different ones but you could see how different springs worked and use a computer screen to see what colour of sofa would best suit the decor of your lounge. You were not an objective bystander who might purchase from the outside, but were yourself involved in the whole process.

IKEA is very *image-driven*, from its logo and store set-up to the style of the furniture. After all, when you go to someone's house for dinner you can spot the IKEA furniture and home goods straight away.

Finally, IKEA is *connected*. Before the arrival of this shop you would go to a kitchen shop to buy a kitchen. IKEA did it differently. You didn't just buy a kitchen but instead looked at a number of mocked-up rooms. Their kitchens were more than warehouse models. They had trinkets and pictures and pans and clocks. They weren't a kitchen to buy off the shelf but instead a kitchen that you could imagine in your house. It was connected as you looked at it, and instead of thinking "Those are nice kitchen cabinets", you thought "That could be my kitchen".

Being EPIC is not restricted to IKEA. Think of other post-modern successes (such as Starbucks or Apple), and the EPIC principles apply strongly. It's also interesting quite how often I'm asked whether it is even possible to have a multi-generational church today. In substance the truth of Jesus is relevant to any age, so really this is purely a question of style. My answer is always the same. If Simon Cowell can create in the *X Factor* a format that works across generations, why can't the church?

This hugely successful TV show regularly attracts a third of the prime-time Saturday-night television audience in the UK. It is the first show in decades that multiple generations of the same family watch together. The really amazing thing is that the format is fundamentally EPIC and yet each generation actually enjoys the programme. No one generation is sacrificing or being inclusive of another; they are all enjoying it and engaging with the format. Each generation may have their favourite, be that an older singer of swing songs in a suit, or a thirty-year-old girl belting out rock songs, or a fresh-faced boy band singing ballads, yet the experience remains shared and fun and engaging for all. It truly is a form of communication that reaches a variety of generations. If Simon Cowell can do this so creatively then why can't the church find a multi-generational model too?

This raises the question of how EPIC our churches are. Sadly, the answer is usually not very, if at all. Our ways of doing things can put people off and push them away from church. In researching *Disappointed with Jesus?* I surveyed just over a hundred young people from Christian backgrounds. Half had left the church and the other half had stayed. Every one of those who had left was not in fact disappointed with Jesus but instead with His church. This cannot continue. We need to create a family and community that pushes people *towards* Jesus, not away from Him.

Our churches may not always be EPIC, but Jesus gives us an amazing example of how to do things. When He was on earth the whole thing was experiential, as He allowed twelve disciples to share life with Him. It was participative, as they were involved throughout (e.g. it was Andrew who brought the little boy's packed lunch to Jesus at the feeding of the five thousand in John 6). It was image-driven, not least at the Last Supper, and it was connected in that the truth of their Rabbi had an impact on every area of their being.

It's time that we as a church became EPIC again and communicated to this generation in a relevant way. After all, it's no use having the greatest message of hope that the world has ever known if your listeners can't access your words, style, and message.

To think about...

- Church is challenging for lots of us in many different ways. We can find comfort in the fact that none of us have found a perfect church – if you think you have that's great, but it might not always feel like that. Church can never be perfect,s as it is made up of imperfect people who all need God to help them.

- Let's not be part of the problem but part of the solution:
  a) Let's not blame Jesus for our own issues.
  b) Let's ask Him how He wants us to look.
  c) Let's act even in the little things – they make a difference.
  d) Let's pray, pray, pray.

CHAPTER 6

Stumbling block:
Broken dreams

(ANNE)

"That's the way it is. It's down there and I'm in here. I guess it comes down to a simple choice, really. Get busy living or get busy dying."

Andy Dufresne, taken from *The Shawshank Redemption*

Marriage partner

As Cara settles down in an easy chair with a steaming cup of tea, she decides not to press the power button on the TV remote control and instead sits back and ponders her life. Living alone, Cara rarely allows herself to dwell on her single status; in fact, she finds it distinctly unhelpful, but tonight she feels cross with the world and frustrated with God. How, she thinks, can I have chosen to follow God all these years and not found a man I can share my life with? How, when it has always been my dream to have a husband and kids, can I be working so hard, feeling so isolated, and living on my own?

As the angry thoughts fill her mind, Cara begins to sob. Deep cries from the core of her being make her body lurch and bend. Tissues are the last thing on her mind – she doesn't care a bit that there is a fast-deepening pool of tears between her feet. Anyway, why *should* she care? It's not as if anyone is around to mop them up. Another wave of sobs racks her body. Yes, there was the word from that prophet guy, Danny, that he said was from God and did, at the time, give her hope of a man in the future. He had made it clear that there would be someone for her later in life – but how late was it going to be? Post-fertility? That would be just so not funny. And anyway wouldn't that mean that she would then marry a divorcé or someone with children? That could produce a whole host of issues that she was not sure she wanted to deal with. After a while, Cara begins to calm down, feeling that she has no tears left to cry.

Instead, she grabs herself a bar of chocolate, always the best option in a crisis, and tries to be thankful. She reassures herself that she has some amazing friends and family, and is incredibly blessed to live where she lives and work where she works. However, deep down, she longs for a great guy and a few children, and feels as if she has been asking for ever. She does not understand why God seems to do miraculous things for others but doesn't answer her cry for a partner. She looks up into the air and cries out to God: "If You really love me and want to give good gifts to me as Your child, then why do I still find myself single? Doesn't Your love mean I get what I want?"

Cara stops dead. "Oh, my word," she concedes. "Somehow I have started to believe that being loved equals getting what I want. And, if I am honest about it, I think I truly have begun to wonder whether God does actually love me – or certainly whether He loves me as much as He loves others."

Despite this insight Cara is still human, and as she snuggles down to sleep that night she finds that she has no answers to the pain of singleness and that she might not have any for a long time, maybe ever. She still cannot get her head around why God has not answered her prayers. And she still faces a ticking biological clock that gets louder every year. She could go to a bar or a sperm bank and get pregnant, but is that really the answer? She could meet a random guy who doesn't love Jesus and get married, but how long would it last? Cara's decision is to keep going and try to keep trusting God even if she doesn't get what she wants, because she has decided that God's love is way bigger than her apparently broken dreams.

Dream job

It was one of those funny moments when you know God is speaking to you but you are struggling to find the guts to share what He has laid on your heart. Neither of us is normally short of words, but when it involves a guy a bit older than us, who has never worn his heart on his sleeve with many people, let alone us, it is very challenging. However, God had clearly spoken to me and when I had eventually plucked up the courage to talk, his reaction made it obvious to us that God was on his case! As his anxieties began to spill out you could see that broken dreams were locked up inside, and no matter how many times he had convinced himself that he was truly blessed, he still had a deep cry in his heart.

For John it was nothing to do with a desire for a partner, as he had an amazing wife and kids; it was that he had always dreamed of being an actor. Just like Cara, though, sobs rose from the core of his being and he struggled to make them stop. John had taken so many odd jobs to try to "make it" in the acting world but eventually he knew that he needed a regular income to support his family. He had ended up in a job he hated in order to pay the mortgage, struggling with a daily desire to be fulfilling his dream instead. Although he was still able to do little bits of theatre, his heart ached to be acting full-time. John felt guilty because he knew he had a great life and that God had given him so much, but he could not shake off this deep desire to act.

As the tears slid down John's face, the reality of his failed pursuit began to strike us. The hours of effort, plethora of failed auditions, and years of doubt had caused him so much pain. He wore an expression of resigned acceptance that the dream of his life was never to be more than a hobby. He had made so many sacrifices for his dream, and felt it was God Himself who had given him a special gift, so he simply could not understand why or how this could be the end of the journey. Was he truly to have a "job" elsewhere as opposed to the vocation he had always felt was from God?

I want to be a footballer

From as early as anyone could remember, Jimmy had been seen with a football. Football was what he loved and every spare moment was spent on this primary passion. Jimmy was a pretty good footballer; in fact, as he grew he turned out to be an excellent one. Throughout his teens he pursued this interest with great enthusiasm. There was plenty of speculation that this might be the career that he would follow. To others this seemed attractive because of the flash cars, luxury villas, and all the other trappings of the millionaire lifestyle. For Jimmy it was attractive simply because, as a professional footballer, he could do the thing he loved the most every day.

Jimmy played at a high level and made many new friends. But it all changed when he got seriously injured. His injury and the resulting investigations revealed a physical weakness that put paid to any hopes of becoming a professional footballer, or playing to any reasonable standard at all. Shattered and destroyed, he knew that he would have to pursue something else. But what else was there? Football meant the world to him.

Fast-forward fifteen years and Jimmy is sitting on the sofa in his lounge watching the football. Just into his early thirties, he looks a far cry from the athlete of his youth. He sits and enjoys watching his beloved England beat current world champions Spain in a match at Wembley. There is a footballer from London playing in central midfield for England that day. This guy puts in a man-of-the-match performance and has just shown that he can dominate a game against the best side in the world. Around 90,000 football fans rock Wembley Stadium with songs of adoration directed at this player. To Jimmy, though, this man is far from a stranger. He is someone he himself played football with for years as a young man.

How differently things have turned out for them both. They had pursued the same dream and been desperate to make it as footballers. They had each had talent and potential. But here they are with very different outcomes – one being paid an insanely high salary to kick a ball around and the other sitting in a lounge in what seems like an entirely different world, watching his former peer being adored. Jimmy can't help wondering where it went wrong and why his dream was shattered while his former teammate has made it to the absolute pinnacle of one of the most competitive worlds around. Jimmy sits there feeling envious of his former teammate while struggling not to shed a tear.

It's so difficult to speak into these situations. Every part of us wanted to go out and shout about John's acting abilities from the rooftops. Every part of us wanted to go out and find Cara the man of her dreams! We wanted Jimmy to have a second chance at football, though for that one it was probably too late! When we realize that we cannot do any of these things, there is quite a challenge ahead. Many people are living with broken dreams. Often they feel these dreams are God-given, and so when they don't come to anything it's a very hard reality to face. It feels as if God Himself has let them down.

Yet sometimes we need to hold on and believe that God knows best. In today's culture, even the idea of waiting goes against the grain. Yet the Bible is full of heroes who were patient and waited. Abraham was incredibly patient, Joseph was in slavery for an awfully long time; indeed, the whole of the Old Testament story is about waiting for the arrival of Jesus the Messiah. Sometimes we simply need to hold on to what we know is true and believe that the unseen God knows best.

Western rites

Part of the problem is that we have a church that says you are weird if you don't get married – you are unusual if you remain single. And so much of what we organize and put on is perfect for married people and families, but very hard for people on their own. This just exacerbates their desire for a partner, because they feel so foreign and lonely. Another part of the problem is that we have a culture that says you can achieve anything if you put your mind to it. Think about recent reality television shows such as *Big Brother*, *The X Factor*, and *American Idol*. They are promoting the idea that you can become famous quite easily – anyone can audition for the shows, and it seems as if all kinds of people from any walk of life can have a shot at fame. The reality is, however, that only a few "make it", and what is "fame" anyway, and why do we value it so highly? The British television and radio presenter Fearne Cotton described it like this: "[The] only difference between being famous and not being famous is that people come up to you in the street that you don't know and they say hello!" Why has our culture become so obsessed with fame?

We cannot overestimate the effect on our society of people dreaming of becoming recognized and famous. As an article in *The Guardian* newspaper pointed out, "Once upon a time, children aspired to be teachers, bankers, doctors. Now they just want to be celebrities."[1] A study of more than 3,000 parents was commissioned for the television show *Tarrant Lets the Kids Loose*. This further proves the point. The study revealed that pre-teens today have very different ideas of what they want to be when they grow up. It showed how much this has changed in recent history. The top three answers today to what children want to be when they grow up are sportsperson (12 per cent), pop star (11 per cent), and actor (11 per cent). These results are strikingly different from those of twenty-five years ago, which were teacher (15 per cent), banker/financier (9 per cent), and doctor/nurse (7 per cent).[2] If we continue to play this fame game then we are in danger of producing an ever-more-superficial society littered with yet more broken dreams.

The Western world promotes the idea that we are all entitled to certain things and we can all have them if we work at it. This is simply not true, and it doesn't just apply to the desire for fame. We faced the same challenge over children: we thought we would get together, get engaged then married, and a little while later have children – as if it was some sort of natural progression for our lives. How strange this would sound to someone in the developing world! And yet the truth is that even if we realize that these things are not just rites of passage, it does not suddenly quench our heart's desire or make us give up hope for good. We can feel tantalized and torn apart by people constantly telling us to "take delight in the Lord, and he will give you the desires of your heart" (Psalm 37:4). It's true, but it doesn't always seem to chime with our everyday reality.

One of our friends says something very helpful on this. In relation to the pain of never having her own children, she says that it is not about giving up hope or longing; it is about trying to find a new hope and a new path of longing. Although her dreams of having children have not been fulfilled, she is determined to have a new dream that will create a new hope within her. It is very challenging stuff, and not for the faint-hearted, but we think there is something powerfully positive about it if you can make it a reality in your life.

There are just some broken dreams in life that do not find neat solutions, and they can keep bringing us to crisis moments and making us wonder whether we really want to continue following God, or even whether we want to follow Him in the first place.

We find Hebrews really helpful here. The kind of "ask and it will be given to you" verses (Matthew 7:7) are a bit too tough in situations like this, but Hebrews seems to be more realistic when we are facing broken dreams. There is something so foreign in our world about holding on to faith no matter what, and yet Hebrews chapter 11, which is often referred to as the "Hall of Faith", greatly commends people who do this:

> By faith Abraham, when called to go to a place he would later receive as his inheritance, obeyed and went, even though he did not know where he was going. By faith he made his home in the promised land like a stranger in a foreign country; he lived in tents, as did Isaac and Jacob, who were heirs with him of the same promise.... For he was looking forward to the city with foundations, whose architect and builder is God...
>
> All these people were still living by faith when they died. They did not receive the things promised; they only saw them and welcomed them from a distance, admitting that they were foreigners and strangers on earth... they were longing for a better country – a heavenly one. Therefore God is not ashamed to be called their God, for he has prepared a city for them.
> (Hebrews 11:8–16, abbreviated)

Some people are so sure of their faith in God that they choose to live by faith even if they do not receive the things promised to them. It is incredible that a relationship with God can be so real and life-changing that it comes above everything else. And that is the story of Cara and John: they have chosen God's way – a way that is still not clear and might never be – ahead of their own personal agendas.

With faith in Jesus we know (more clearly than those such as Abraham and Sarah) that we have eternal life and that He has prepared a place for us (John 14:1–3) – so, even though life is challenging, it is short and we will go somewhere far more amazing for eternity. In John 10 verse 29 Jesus says that we will not be snatched out of God's hand – we belong to Him and will be with Him for ever. Whatever happens – whether our dreams become a reality on earth or not – the constant challenge is: will we have faith to keep going right now? Or will this stumbling block succeed in sapping away all our hope in God?

We only ever see a small part of what is going on. Our view is often only of what is directly in front of us, and not the whole picture that God sees. Therefore there must be a way of finding the strength to trust that He actually knows best. This is easy to say, but we do need to try. We need to believe that God's plans for us truly are the best, and that when He says the following words in Jeremiah 29:11 He does mean them:

> "For I know the plans I have for you," declares the LORD, "plans to prosper you and not to harm you, plans to give you hope and a future."

Things might not turn out as we predict, but God knows best. We must trust Him and not allow our broken dreams to become the obstacles that knock us off course. After all, "Jimmy" is in fact Gavin, and though he may still dream of playing football for England (as two of his former teammates have), were Gavin a footballer, he could not be the head of Youth for Christ. God's plan was different, and Gavin is a much better leader of YFC than he ever would have been a footballer – and don't let him ever convince you otherwise!

To think about...

- What do you truly long for? Have all your dreams been realized or are some of them deeply buried within you? No matter how long you have waited, keep being real with Jesus about these dreams. He still listens, even if you are struggling to hope any more.

- We never know what lies around the corner – and must never presume we do. God is a God of surprises. They might not be as you predicted but they will be life-changing.

- Is there a new path of dreaming/longing that you could take that might shift your focus and unleash fresh hope in you?

CHAPTER 7

Stumbling block:
When life is bad

(GAVIN AND ANNE)

"Happiness can be found, even in the darkest of times, if one only remembers to turn on the light."

Albus Dumbledore, taken from *Harry Potter and the Prisoner of Azkaban*[1]

Nothing, no one, nowhere, prepared me for the news that we were about to hear. So far, life had been pretty great. I had met the man of my dreams, he loved God, he loved me, and we had got married on a beautiful day of celebration. We had bought a small house; we had started working at Youth for Christ, and found a real support network and place to serve God. We had an incredible marriage, a loving church, and great parents and wider family. All the boxes were ticked except for one: children. For some reason I honestly believed that because God had done so much for us He would, when we decided we were ready, provide us with a family. There was a huge part of me that thought it was just another rite of passage – you get engaged, you get married, and then you have children. On top of that was this strange notion that when you commit your life to serving God, life gets easier; it falls into place, and becomes in a way "complete". Surely, with God in our life, the best we envisaged would always come to pass if we prayed hard enough?

But after two years of trying to have a baby, nothing had happened. To try to find out what was going wrong, we went for tests.

****

I vividly remember the week we found out the results of those fertility tests. I had felt sorry for Anne for ages because there was clearly something wrong with her and she would soon know the extent of her infertility. We found out Anne's results first. Unless there was a problem the doctor's receptionist could tell you the results over the phone. Anne was very nervous and as she held the phone it shook manically in her grasp. I knew that I had to help, so I grabbed the handset and rang for her. I'm usually very confident, but as I held the phone I could feel my whole body tensing up with anxiety. I pulled myself together and dialled the number.

"Everything is clear with your wife's tests, Mr Calver," the receptionist politely informed me. Anne and I felt a great sense of relief.

Two days later it was my turn. Strangely, I was far less nervous for myself than I had been for Anne. I confidently rang the receptionist and was somewhat surprised when she said, "You need to make an appointment with the doctor straight away, Mr Calver. In fact there is one available in fifteen minutes' time, if you would like it?" In shock we took the appointment and, with very little time to think, arrived at the surgery in a whirl.

We walked gingerly into Consultation Room Four and took seats facing a computer screen full of statistics. The doctor was doing her level best to look hopeful, but before she said anything I saw something that made my heart sink. The screen was full of white text but at the top under my name was written "sperm sample". Poorly camouflaged amid the white text was one red word in bold capital letters that read: **ABNORMAL**. What on earth did this mean? What was going to happen? For the first time I genuinely realized that it could actually be me who had the problem. Throughout this process I had secretly assumed that Anne was the one who was stalling things.

The doctor spoke up. "Thanks for coming in. I'm afraid that it's not all good news. Gavin, you are not sterile, but neither can you be considered fertile. Your sperm have low motility – fundamentally, they are lazy," she said.

"What on earth does that mean?" I thought. She explained it all statistically and said that we had an outside chance of conceiving, but that equally we might never have a baby. Had we been thirty-five years old and not in our twenties then we would have had no chance, she added. I couldn't believe what I was hearing. I had a problem. It was because of me that Anne wasn't pregnant. How could this be? Again I thought that all around me were stories of fourteen-year-olds getting pregnant, abortions, and abandoned children, yet we might never have one. It all seemed so unfair.

Infertility is a reality for so many couples, but I didn't pause to ask why we should be any different from them. All we did was to leave the surgery and go home. It was Friday afternoon and the whole weekend was horrible. Preaching twice on the Sunday was a particular strain. I meant every word that I proclaimed, but I probably thought about it more than usual and it certainly cost me to preach on the glory of God and His bountiful provision that day.

Over the next forty-eight hours the dust settled a little. I was really hurting. Anne was great about it and reassured me that she'd rather have no children and me than us not be together, but it still killed me inside. It broke my heart every time I looked at her. I knew how much she wanted a baby, and yet because she had chosen me she might never have one. That was enough to break me. I'm very much the alpha male and just expected reproduction to happen. After all, I've always fixed things, yet here was something I could do nothing about. All of a sudden I felt like half a man. Surely the most natural thing is for a man to spread his seed, and if I couldn't do that then what kind of failure did that make me?

We knew we needed some help, so we told a few people who were close to us, as we were desperate for both prayer and support. We sat down with one particular couple. As we shared, they listened intently. We often do the listening in our relationships, but today it was obvious that we needed to be heard. Eventually the wife spoke up.

"With all you do for Jesus, the lives you lead, the miles you travel, the sacrifices you've undertaken, has this made you question Him, His goodness and existence?"

Impulsively I said, "No way!" What a strange question, I thought to myself.

****

I hit a roadblock. Even though I knew I loved Gav with all my heart and wanted to be with him until the day I died, I had this horrible pain inside – and I knew he felt responsible. Gavin felt it was unfair but all I could think was "Did God *really* love me? Because if He did, wouldn't He give me a baby?"

Unbelievably, and shockingly after hearing the news that we probably couldn't have a baby, we fell pregnant the very next month. I don't write that lightly or with any superiority, because I know it is not the reality for many. However, it happened to us, and it was the weirdest set of emotions – going from totally devastated to completely elated in the space of a few weeks was crazy. The roadblock came tumbling down and in its place was an exciting but rather rocky road. At thirty-six weeks we were told that a "little c" antibody was attacking the baby and could cause anaemia. Because they had picked it up so late and the levels were not too high, I was able to get to thirty-nine weeks before they induced me and delivered Amelie Hope Calver into my arms. It was incredible.

****

After all we had been through it was the most amazing thing to meet Amelie. She was beautiful yet fiery. I was genuinely overwhelmed by what the Lord had done for us. Here we were, just ten months on from such incredible pain, with the most amazing baby. The whole thing had happened in such a whirlwind. From my bad results, to the night I was quietly watching Arsenal v Juventus in the Champions League and Anne went to the toilet and came back to announce her pregnancy, to the moment that I met my daughter and held her in my arms for the first time. What a journey.

****

Amelie was a total joy but also a deep challenge for me. To go from being out and about and pretty much living life how I wanted to suddenly being responsible for a baby, and having her demands dictate my day, was a huge challenge. I mean, how on earth was I supposed to find time for a relationship with Jesus when I was totally shattered and emotional? When we did a positive pregnancy test eleven months later it was another shock – one half of me was not ready to have another baby but the other part said, "Wow, another miracle; God is incredible – He has taken the doctors' truth and trampled it under His feet!"

When I started to bleed at six weeks I thought it was all going to be fine. We went to the hospital just to be on the safe side, but I knew that plenty of people bleed, especially early in pregnancy. They covered me with the familiar cold jelly and then ran the scanner over my lower tummy. When we saw the tiny baby before our eyes, we froze in shock. There was definitely the formation of a tiny body but there was no movement and no sound of a heartbeat. I knew somehow deep in my guts that my child had died.

****

As a man, when you go to a baby scan you do your best to understand and be interested. There you are, making out you can see the baby and that although it looks like something between a raisin and a mushroom it is cute! So there I was making out that I could see the baby and that it was obviously cute when the reality hit that this was an ultrasound scan with no sound. The midwife gently informed us that our baby had no heartbeat and had died in the womb. I was immediately devastated. I felt that I could deal with miracle babies or even no babies, but not this. Such false hope was something I was not prepared for.

I could feel my mind filling with questions: why has this happened? Who is playing with us? Why couldn't it all be OK? We came out of the room and Amelie (who was eighteen months old) hugged my leg. I immediately sensed the Lord saying to me, "Be faithful to Me as I have been faithful to you. Don't ask Me for what you don't have, but be grateful for what you *do* have." In that moment I felt an overwhelming gratitude once more for Amelie and a sense that I needed to dust myself down and be there for the family. I did have a painful chapter ahead of me. I wasn't pretending not to hurt, but I was determined to fight on.

****

"Mrs Calver, we can't tell you what to do, but you should think about having a D and C [an operation to remove the baby]." There was a chance that the baby would come away naturally but it could take a while and be a painfully long process. In a state of shock and on a roller coaster of emotions, I agreed to have the operation the next day. It was the loneliest day of my life. I remember saying to God as I lay on the hospital bed, "Why is all this happening to me? When can it be over? Please take away the pain." Gone was the sense of life being easy with God, and in its place was a desperate reaching out to something greater than myself.

I didn't want to get pregnant ever again. I was terrified of losing another baby; I was worried about the antibodies they had picked up in my body at the end of the pregnancy with Amelie. I felt as if I couldn't cope with any more pain for a long time. I think when you experience fear like that you will do anything to make things calm down and for peace to resume. All you want is for life to return to "normal", and that's definitely what I was longing for. So we kept putting off the decision and I tried to put it to bed. And yet there was this strange nagging at the back of my head, some would say God(!), that constantly said, "Anne, you need to stare fear in the face and overcome it... don't let it dictate your life." I tried to ignore the voice and focus on the fact that the doctors had said that we wouldn't have any children, and how amazing it was that we had one beautiful daughter – and we should leave it at that. But something kept making me question and wonder, "What if we tried again?" Isn't it frustrating when you can't make something lie down in your mind and, just when you think you are moving on, it keeps rearing its ugly head? The bottom line was that I knew that the journey of having another baby might be terrifying, but – and it was a big "but" – it could be life-changing too.

STUMBLING
BLOCKS

****

That autumn we nervously decided to try for another child. Nothing could have prepared us for what lay ahead! Anne got pregnant almost straight away. By this stage I had started to accept that I had at some point been healed of my fertility problem! I had been forward for prayer so often and here I was, having got Anne pregnant three times in four years. I could hardly claim to have a problem in this area any more.

We were really looking forward to a holiday in the USA with my family over Thanksgiving in November. We had never been over there for that uniquely American celebration and we were keen for Amelie to experience something different. It was the night before we were to go on one of those stupidly early flights, the type that guarantees you get no sleep the night before out of fear of sleeping through the 4 a.m. alarm. The type that, as the great British comedian Michael McIntyre famously says, you feel the need to constantly point out to others! You insist on telling anyone who will listen that you are getting up at *4 a.m.*!

The poor car was packed to overflowing with a full load testing its suspension on our drive – we were all set. It was about 9:30 at night and, having finally finished getting ready and checked the passports and tickets more times than I care to remember, we settled down with a relaxing drink before our few hours' kip. I can remember that we were watching the first night of the somewhat crass British television show *I'm a Celebrity... Get Me Out of Here!* During one of the many advert breaks Anne popped upstairs to go to the loo. A few moments later I heard what sounded like tears and gentle sobbing from upstairs. I shouted up and sure enough Anne was really upset. I could feel her pain for myself as she said sharply, "I'm bleeding."

We had no idea what to do next. It felt as if our world was caving in around us, and we were about to go to the other side of the world. We were in a spin and desperately in need of reassurance and some idea of what to do. One of our friends was a specialist in this fertility medical stuff, so we rang him. His advice was helpful and direct: we should not be going on a plane or anything like that but instead should go to the hospital in the morning. We looked at each other bleakly, entirely at a loss as to what to do next. We knew we couldn't go anywhere, yet we were all packed up and had even given our neighbour the remains from the fridge. We got into bed for a restless night of tossing and turning, unaware of what the next day might bring. I will never forget lying in bed that night in a state of shock, pleading with God to help us. I prayed that same desperate prayer all night long.

Finally the night was over and morning was upon us. The first thing that hit me was Amelie. She had been so excited the night before as we put her to bed with the promise of a flight the next morning. She couldn't wait to get on a plane and go and see Grandma and Grandpa, and had taken an age to fall asleep herself. The hardest thing was facing her the next morning. The excitement in her young eyes as she saw us was quickly wiped away as we had to painfully let her know that we weren't going on a plane to New York and instead needed to go to the hospital in Dudley. She didn't understand, but was amazingly gracious about it all.

We took Anne's car to the hospital, as neither of us could face my car full of winter woolies, travel cot, and presents. The journey seemed to take an age and we were all relieved when it was finally over and we pulled up at the hospital. In something of a daze we headed for the early pregnancy section that was now so familiar to us. As we walked along the small corridors many emotions were quickly coming back to the surface, not least the fact that the last time we had been there we had lost a baby.

Anne was scanned quickly and to our immense delight the baby seemed to be doing well. We were so relieved and joyful that things seemed to be OK. In addition to this we were taken to see the specialist. It was here that we were reminded of the antibody problems that were possibly going to affect things. We went into a meeting with a consultant and he was somewhat perplexed by the nature of the problems. He actually said it was all a bit beyond him, and wished us all the best as he passed us into the care of the leading specialist in the country, based at the Birmingham Women's Hospital. This was all a lot to take in, but at least the specialist was based just a few miles from home.

We went home feeling greatly relieved and yet also a little put out. Here we were, back in Halesowen with a car full of holiday luggage to unpack and two weeks to spend at home. Even if we could have rearranged flights and stuff, we had been advised not to travel. We were so blessed that day as friends did a food shop and others supported us, but it was hard not to feel sorry for ourselves. We felt so grateful at this juncture that the baby had survived, but we had no idea of the pressures and trauma that lay ahead.

Anne went into the new hospital every couple of weeks and things seemed to be going OK. We were told that at some point there would probably need to be some kind of intervention, but for the time being things were looking fine. It was particularly great when Anne went for a check-up just before Christmas and they said things were good and to enjoy the festive season.

We had a good Christmas and were looking forward to celebrating New Year and all that 2010 would hold. But Anne had another check-up on 30 December and this time things couldn't have been more different. On the scan, our seventeen-

and-a-half-week-old baby was hardly moving and there were noticeable amounts of fluid around the organs. The roomful of medics was silent as they considered the levels of antibodies in the blood and how seriously anaemic the baby was. Filling out forms and signing things allowing almost immediate intervention with great risks to a very poorly tiny baby was horrendous.

We were told that they would need to do a blood transfusion *in utero* on New Year's Eve. Horrible timing! We were dumbfounded by the news and I sat there transfixed by the tiny life hardly moving on the screen in front of me. They can only do such interventions from eighteen weeks, and these are very rare and carry quite a risk. We knew we had a fight on our hands for this life that could so easily slip away. We found ourselves pleading with God to take care of our baby in its own lions' den, knowing that the next twenty-four hours would change our lives for ever.

****

Before that first transfusion, I was a mess. I remember breaking down in the Tesco car park and feeling utterly terrified, broken, and the weakest I had ever felt. Gavin had to take Amelie out of the car and into the supermarket because I was such a wreck. I couldn't believe this was happening to me. What was going on? How were we going to get through this? In that moment I knew I had to find a way to carry on with the journey. I reached out for God.

Some people at a time like that would turn their backs on God, feeling that He had abandoned them or that He didn't care, or demanding to know why He was letting them go through this. I can understand all those responses, but for some reason I didn't do that. I just fell into His arms in total desperation.

I pleaded with Jesus, "Please, God, will You make me, not break me, through this? Please help me to trust You through everything, no matter what happens; please give me the strength to walk every day because I cannot do this on my own."

I could see Gavin and Amelie in the mirror, returning to the car. The mirror also helpfully revealed black circles all round my eyes and streaking down my face. In that minute I wiped my eyes as best I could, clung on to God inside, and composed myself. And I think that was the key: I didn't just squish down what was going on inside me; I threw it onto God and prayed that I would be real and deal with the emotion as and when it came up, and not fall apart later because I hadn't faced the reality as it was happening.

Amelie was deeply concerned by my earlier reaction but I was able to encourage her and explain briefly why I was upset. Gavin and I told her that the baby was poorly and that we needed to pray lots that the little life would be OK. She slowly became calmer as she saw us settle our minds a bit.

After a terrible sleepless night, tossing and turning, praying and hoping, churning and yearning, we returned to the hospital. When they took me through to be scanned again, I was surprised but the comment came back: "We need to check your baby is still OK before we operate." Basically they were checking to see if it was still alive – scary. In that moment, as they put the scanner on my stomach for what already felt like the millionth time, I just had to ask what sex my child was. If we lost this baby I wanted to know if we would be mourning a girl or a boy. The midwife showed me clearly on the screen that it was a boy (!) – I think in my gut I had known that all along, but the confirmation was helpful. It was a bittersweet couple of minutes as we rejoiced in the idea of having a son as well as a daughter but then felt a heaviness descend fast – this operation could as easily be the end of his life as the beginning. The risks were extreme.

Off I went to the ward, got changed into a delightful "backless" patient gown, and took the sedatives. Thank the Lord for sedatives – for me, it took the edge off everything that was happening. For Gav, it was different.

****

The transfusion itself was quite an experience. As it was so early in the pregnancy, the potential risks and dangers were high. Our condition was exceptionally rare and we were studied by Cambridge University. Additionally, we were informed that there were only a couple of donors on the national blood register who had the right blood.

The medics managed to locate the right blood and Anne was wheeled down to theatre. I sat by her bed nervously as they spent what seemed like an eternity prepping everything. Finally, we were ready. There was a monitor for me to stare at as the live images of what was taking place started to scroll before my eyes. There was our son, barely moving and not looking too good, in Anne's womb.

Eventually it all began and they stuck a needle into Anne's belly and through into her womb and finally into our boy. At such an early stage they needed to put it into the baby's stomach as no vein was mature enough to take a needle. They took some blood out of the baby and as it came out into the syringe it didn't look like the blood I was used to seeing; in fact it looked like slightly pink water. I was deeply troubled by this, as it was the first clear sign that he was really in trouble.

Then it was time to put in the new blood. They filled the syringes and delicately started to put new blood into our baby's stomach. On the screen the needle looked like a sparkler, and as the new blood poured in it fizzled. The whole thing was an amazing image of new life as this blood sparkled its way into our son's system. In the end it was all over fairly quickly. Anne was sedated and I was told that she would need to sleep it all off, and we would know if it had been a success in a few hours' time.

"How?" I asked.

One of the midwives took me aside. "The biggest risk to your baby at this stage is a cardiac arrest due to pumping that much blood in at such a young age. If your baby is OK in a few hours' time then we'll know that there has been no heart attack, and we can all move forward and fight on."

The next few hours were awful. I can't recall ever feeling as alone as I did sitting next to Anne's bed with her out of it all. Anne looked so still, peaceful, and beautiful, yet I felt that I was going through the wringer. I felt so afraid, so weak, so lonely, so helpless. I felt compelled to pray. The only comfort I could find was in Jesus. Many would later ask me, "Where was Jesus?", and I could say that in my moment of great strife He was simply there with me.

I prayed a simple prayer: "Lord Jesus, if this baby lives, You are good, and if this baby dies, You are still good. Either way I'm going to wake up tomorrow and proclaim that You are good." It was so hard to pray and I struggled to get every single syllable out. But I was determined. The question for me was not "Why does God allow suffering?", but instead "Where is God when we suffer?" I found the answer in the loneliness of that clinical room – He's with us, holding our hand.

****

Our baby survived that first transfusion, and ten days later we went through it all again, ten days after that again, and again – nine blood transfusions in the womb and then a further four outside. Every week, often twice a week, I had to go into Fetal

Medicine and be scanned and monitored. One time at about twenty-eight weeks they were struggling with the trace (picking up a consistent heartbeat), so I was admitted for the night. Later on, upstairs in the ward, they couldn't find the heartbeat at all, and everyone went into a total frenzied panic. I was rushed at full speed down to theatre and was hastily prepared for a Caesarean section.

I felt so alone and unsure – I had no idea how this was going to turn out, so all I did was close my eyes and reach for God again (for the millionth time). For some reason, before they operated they allowed two of my friends from church into the preparation room (they had been visiting me on the ward when it all kicked off). The two of them began to pray for me and, as they did, the most amazing thing happened: the baby's heartbeat began to pick up and then steady, so that by the time the doctor reappeared with his crew ready to do the C-section, they could not understand what on earth had gone on. I stayed in that room all night giving thanks for my friends' timely arrival and that the baby didn't need to be delivered at twenty-eight weeks!

Amazingly, I made it to thirty-one and a half weeks before they delivered Daniel. I was pleased that the professor who had done all the transfusions was then able to deliver my son as well. Granted, I couldn't hold him in my arms for over a week, but seeing the professor pull Daniel out of the womb, hold him up in pride, and quickly show him to me was one of the most dramatic and moving memories I will carry with me for the rest of my life. Daniel had some excellent intensive care and was able to come home at thirty-six weeks old – a total miracle.

Although the next four months were tough – watching Daniel's health deteriorate and taking him back into hospital for four more transfusions – we were just so thrilled to have the gift of a baby boy. I could not have got through it without my faith and without the phenomenal and consistent support of our church all over the world, our families, and our close friends.

Coming out the other side

What a journey the whole thing was. I prayed that same prayer by Anne's bed about God being good on each of the nine times that our baby had a blood transfusion in the womb. Each time there was a happy ending, but I'm hopeful that if there had been a bad one I could still have prayed the same prayer and meant it. It's fascinating how instant the loss of faith is for so many. The day the girl dumps you, so goes faith; the day of the letter of redundancy, there goes the faith too. It's as if the instant culture we live in has taken over faith as well. This whole adventure taught me that God's goodness is the same in good and bad. We must stand strong in times of struggle.

It was such a relief to finally meet the little man we had previously only seen on a screen. He was tiny, and as the expert professor who had cared so well for him pulled him out into the world our son marked his entrance suitably by weeing all over him. We were not allowed to hold him and he was rushed away, but at least he had made it into the world. What a fighter of a little man he was proving to be.

The next few weeks and months were spent staring at our son while he was attached to many wires in a plastic box, followed by numerous hospital visits for further care. He was born on 9 April and it was not hard to name him Daniel – after all, we had been praying for our son in a lions' den for quite some time. Incredibly, on 31 August 2010 he was given the all-clear. His problems had always been blood-related and the human body replaces all its blood cells every three to six months. He now had only his own blood, and so was better. Amazing!

****

I think that when you go through a tough time, you have a choice of how to respond. You could think, "Woe is me; why do I have to go through this? If God loved us then it wouldn't happen to us" (and that's how I began this journey). But the reality is that every single one of us goes through challenges – whether we have faith in God or not. Faith, in my experience, is not some sort of protective security blanket that stops problems and pain affecting our life; it is belief in a person who journeys through it with us. And that person is not just any person; that person is God – who has the power to strengthen us and uphold us through everything – someone we can turn to at any point during the day or night, regardless of the situation.

Pain and struggles can stop us from following God. So many of us blame God when things go wrong, or struggle to walk on with Him when we have been battered and bruised by life, but surely it is not God's fault?

I love the "treasures in jars of clay" bit in the Bible (2 Corinthians chapter 4, particularly verses 7b, 8, and 9): "This all-surpassing power is from God and not from us. We are hard pressed on every side, but not crushed; perplexed, but not in despair; persecuted, but not abandoned; struck down, but not destroyed." Whatever we have to face, we don't have to face it on our own, and it doesn't have to write us off. With God's power at work in us we can carry on and overcome and be changed more into His likeness.

Don't get me wrong: I don't think this means that life then feels easy or that we don't have any negative thoughts or feelings – that is just not reality. It simply means that we are not alone, we have a God we can put our trust in and rely on, and we can come out of the valley stronger than when we went in. The words of Matt Redman's song "You Never Let Go" were poignant to me through the journey with Daniel. It says:

Even though I walk through the valley of the shadow of death,
your perfect love is casting out fear,
and even when I'm caught in the middle of the storms of this life,
I won't turn back; I know you are near."[2]

(Extract taken from the song "You Never Let Go" by Matt & Beth Redman, Copyright © 2005 Thankyou music)

I could genuinely relate to this. The love of Jesus can penetrate our hearts so much that our fear lessens – as we cling to His love, He holds on to us and challenges us. How do people face things like this without God?

So often pain turns people away from God, but surely it should instead turn us back towards Him, not create a stumbling block that makes us give up. After all, He doesn't owe us anything, does He?

To think about...

- Whatever pain we have faced or are facing, we always have the choice as to how to respond. Sometimes it is so traumatic we choose things we wish we never had. God is still a God of abundant grace and when we come home to Him He receives us with open arms.

- You can let pain change you or cripple you.
  You can let it make you or break you.
  You can blame God, or you can somehow in your agony ask for His help.

  He is waiting.

CHAPTER 8

Stumbling block:
Christianity feels mundane

(GAVIN AND ANNE)

"Love withers with predictability; its very essence is surprise and amazement. To make love a prisoner of the mundane is to take its passion and lose it forever."

Leo Buscaglia

Do you ever wonder how helpful it is for kids to grow up in a Christian home? It has always been one of those things that we thought was only good, and to be honest, in the main, it still is. However, it may sound strange to say it but we do think there are some negatives. We can't count the number of twenty-somethings who, after hearing one of our testimonies, have come up to us and said, "Oh, I wish I had rebelled in my teens, like you!" And we are thinking, "Surely not? Why on earth would you wish you had done things that you might later repent of?" But some do seem to have a genuine regret that they grew up in a Christian home with a clear set of values and boundaries, which they stuck to at every turn. Not because they don't think those values are good, but because it never exposed them to anything different.

It seems to many that there is something overly familiar

about Christianity. Yes, it's true, but it just seems so mundane when juxtaposed with the exciting testimony in which someone else appears to have lived a bit and then met Jesus. It can sometimes seem unfair that others have this Hollywood-style conversion story that gets everyone hyped up and excited, while the individual who has ploughed along faithfully is left with no story and a seemingly monotonous journey of non-rebellious conformity.

Encounter

Growing up – Anne on the Wirral, Gavin in London – we each had a number of different friends. We both had friends who believed in God and friends who didn't. Gav had one mate whom he was quite close to. Anyone would say that this boy had an incredible upbringing, with loving parents and siblings who followed God and who went to church every week. He had a good set of mates and was able to find a way to live as a Christian even through adolescence and beyond: every parent's dream of a perfect friend! Gavin, on the other hand (clearly not influenced enough by his friend!), walked away from the church in his teens and enjoyed the party life, so when he really met Jesus at eighteen it was incredibly powerful and life-changing. The reason for this was that he knew clearly what he had been saved from. He had seen what life without God was like and knew that it would not bring him lasting fulfilment. He was sure that people would let him down, no matter how well he did at football or what he did to prove himself, and it became very obvious to him just how messed up the world was. When Gav went looking for God he knew he was looking for more, and when he met Jesus he found something that was totally awe-inspiring and it made him adamant that he would never live for anything or anyone else but Jesus.

His mate's reaction was fascinating. Although really happy for Gav that he had become a Christian, he was also frustrated and confused. He had thought he would be totally thrilled and would welcome him home with open arms; after all, he had seen the mess Gav had made of his teenage years and had witnessed him getting into situations that brought hurt and pain. But deep down inside him it was tough.

One day he turned to Gav and said, "There is a part of me that envies how massively this is changing your life. How come you can mess up that badly and yet have such a powerful encounter with God?"

Really what he was saying was, "How come *I* have followed Jesus all these years and been so obedient, and yet not had an experience like yours?" It can seem so unfair that a rebel can turn around in an instant and receive the same grace as a faithful follower. But then grace isn't fair, is it? We don't get what we deserve, but instead so very much more.

Over the months that passed Gavin kept assuring him that he wished he had behaved better and understood the love of God in a way that he could reconcile with being a teenager, but he hadn't been able to. It did not matter how many times he told his friend that he would have preferred to live as a Christian throughout those years; it was still tough for him to observe Gav's dramatic encounter with God: he had wept, heard God speak audibly, realized what a sinner he was and how much he needed a Saviour, and his life was changed beyond recognition in a very short time. His friend, on the other hand, had always known God's love for him and had never left his Father's house. So at times it was that much harder for him to understand what it was that he had been "saved" from.

The older son

The above story really reminds us of the biblical story of the prodigal son. In so many ways we have wondered why the older son is not just thrilled to see his younger brother come home. After all, both of us can relate in many ways to the younger son, but struggle to grasp the older son's perspective. Why is he not helping his father to dress his brother in the finest robes? Why is he not joining in the banquet instead of questioning what his brother has done? And yet when we reflect on what Gav witnessed with one of his closest friends, we get a clearer idea of why he had questions to ask, and Henri Nouwen's powerful words from his writings on Rembrandt's famous painting *The Return of the Prodigal Son* clearly highlight the feelings from the "other side":

> It is strange to say this but deep in my heart, I have known the feeling of envy toward the wayward son. It is the emotion that arises when I see my friends having a good time doing all sorts of things I condemn... I often wonder why I didn't have the nerve to do some of it or all of it myself. The obedient and dutiful life of which I am proud or for which I am praised feels, sometimes, like a burden that was laid on my shoulders and continues to oppress me, even when I have accepted it to such a degree that I cannot throw it off.[1]

You can understand why he would question his father's treatment of the younger son if he feels like this, and why it would cause frustration and confusion in his mind. After all, the younger son returns after squandering his father's money and living life "to the full", and yet it is as if he is being rewarded for this behaviour!

How dare Gav's meeting with his heavenly Father be so incredible when he had done just what the younger son had done! However, the passage is fascinating because when the father explains why he is celebrating with his younger son he says, "My son, you are always with me, and everything I have is yours. But we had to celebrate and be glad, because this brother of yours was dead and is alive again; he was lost and is found" (Luke 15:31–32).

Interestingly, Gav's friend is still in his Father's house, but wouldn't it be fascinating if Jesus had continued the story of the lost son and we got to hear what happened to the older son and whether he was able to stay in his father's house and still know that that was the best place to be? We wonder if he would really begin to know the value of being in the house and of not doing what his brother had chosen to do. Henri Nouwen believes that the older son is lost like the younger son, just in a different way: "Just as I do not know how the younger son accepted the celebration or how he lived with his father after his return, I also do not know whether the elder son ever reconciled himself with his brother, his father or himself."[2]

It is *so* challenging! We can be living as a Christian, growing up in a Christian home, and sticking with God over the years, and yet still be confronted with the stumbling block of the younger son. Sticking with faith definitely presents its challenges – they are totally different from the ones facing those who walk away from God and then eventually come home, but they are very real and may not have the same consequences as for my friend. The pain of seeing the return of the prodigals might sometimes be too much to bear.

Another prodigal

Interestingly, it also happens another way. We know many people who have disappeared from church and come back later, like the lost son, but then there are also those who journey through church, like Gav's friend, but then decide to leave when they are much older. It's almost as if they have finally found a way out! These stories sadden us greatly, as it often seems that they have tried but somehow not had a real encounter or enough of one to make them want to stay.

One of Anne's close friends grew up going to church. Like Gav's friend, he was committed to church life, he was involved with the music group, and he faithfully went to every group that church provided for his age. He prayed, he read the Bible, and he sang Christian songs. While Anne was out drinking and dating, he stayed at home and made his parents proud. They always knew where he was, whom he was with, and what he was doing. He had a good group of Christian friends and a couple of relatively innocent relationships with nice Christian girls. His parents had nothing to worry about – he worked hard at school and excelled in everything he did. Like Gavin's mate, Anne's friend was committed to church life and remained "in his Father's house" in every sense of the phrase.

However, when he left to go to university, things began to change. Suddenly he was exposed to a whole new way of living; it was as if the world was opened up to him for the first time. He had friends from different faith backgrounds; he met people with completely different life experiences and they fascinated him – more than that, they showed him a different way to live. Whereas Gavin's friend had gone to university and got immersed in church and small groups to keep his faith going, Anne's mate did not. While Anne was busy building an incredibly life-changing relationship with God, her friend was heading down a different path. The Christian Union seemed irrelevant to him and the adventure of hedonistic university life so much more appealing than the monotony of church. He made different choices and ultimately, over a long period, decided to give up on God. He is a prodigal who hasn't yet returned.

A narrow view

Are we sometimes at risk of sheltering our children too much? Are we in a position where we can teach Christian values and boundaries to such an extent that we prevent our young people from discovering the truth of Jesus for themselves? I wonder whether we make being a Christian so "normal" that it loses some of its wonder. Perhaps we are in danger of wrapping them up in a Christian bubble where they think that following God is the norm, so they do it, but never really know why until it's too late. Is it fair to say that some "Christians" are lost, even if they are still in their Father's house? It makes sense of why some actually do leave. Did Gav's friend really ever know (until after Gav's encounter) what he was saved from, or had he just accepted a world view and remained committed to it?

If we think for a minute about David Beckham's children growing up in the world they are in. For many years all they will know and understand is that they have money and they are provided for in every way. They will grow up surrounded by cameras and get used to seeing their faces in the media. They will have a very specific understanding of fame, and their response to it all will be interesting to see. Will they choose to follow the path of football or fashion? Will they want to keep the fame and acquire their own in their own right, or will they perhaps want to get as far away from it as possible? One could argue that, to us, fame is an exciting thing that lots of people long for, but children like them see a totally different side. Fame is not exciting to the Beckham children; it's their normal everyday reality. You could also argue that for someone finding faith for the first time and realizing that they are a child of

God it is the most exciting thing they have discovered, but for those growing up in a Christian home, has that wonder grown cold? Was that wonder ever actually there? For those nurtured into faith with no obvious moment of salvation, things can be so different. Will their lack of exposure to the realities of life eventually stop them from choosing to live for Jesus? As a young person moves from the concrete understandings of childhood into the abstract realms, what happens to their view on how life began?

Our own children are growing up in a secure Christian home, and as much as that is the best sort of background they could have, where they know that they are deeply loved, it is also a challenge to know how to communicate Jesus to them. We do not want them to end up giving up on following Him because they haven't had a chance to try anything else, and yet if it is possible we would rather they didn't have to rebel as we did. Equally, we don't want them simply to inherit our faith, as that would never last. We want them both to discover an authentic relationship of their own with Jesus. Our hearts' cry is that they would at some point know the reality of moving from death to life and lost to found in a deep and life-changing way without having to go through the experience of the lost son or the pain of the older one. We do not want them ever to feel like the older son towards a friend or family member. Neither do we want them ever to feel obliged to go the way their parents have gone or to follow Jesus just because "that's what you do". Lord, help us!

The carpenter's son

Picture the scene in Nazareth: people in the village wandering around with dusty feet, collecting water from the well, picking up simple bits of food, and stopping to chat to passers-by.

A few children run past – one of them is Jesus. How do the gossiping adults respond? "Wonder what they are up to?" we can hear them say. To them, Jesus would have been just Mary and Joseph's boy – no one special – just a child playing with his friends. In Nazareth Jesus was part of the furniture, just like anyone else. He wasn't perceived as different – He wasn't wealthy; He didn't have royal status (in the way that people would understand); He was a carpenter's son. No wonder He says that "only in his home town and in his own house is a prophet without honour" (Matthew 13:57).

The great Christian communicator Rob Parsons picks up on this:

> The good folk of Nazareth had just got too used to Jesus. They saw Him every day. When they were young they had played with Him in the dusty streets, and later on they had gone to His father's workshop to get the yokes for their oxen made. There was nothing new you could tell them about Him."[3]

It is possible to get too used to Jesus, and for Him not to be rightly revered because we see Him as so "everyday". We must be really wary of this.

With Jesus in our lives from a very young age, with the children's Bible in the bookcase from the year dot, saying grace before a meal, and listening to Christian songs, we can lose some of the power of what the cross of Christ really means for our lives. Having cross-stitch pictures with Bible verses on the walls and Christian conversations happening all over the house makes Jesus seem normal. In our lives today, growing up in a Christian home can become like it was in Nazareth – "Oh, that's just Jesus; He is always here." We can find that we are so familiar with Jesus that we can get bored by Him and go looking for people or things that seem more exciting. Did those people from His home town really understand what happened when Jesus went to the cross and rose again, or was He still "just Jesus"? Did they get what it meant for them for the rest of their lives?

We must not let familiarity with Jesus breed contempt in our understanding of Him. He is the Saviour of the world, and this must never become mundane. We try to pray every day, "Lord, show us what we are saved from," as we long for it to remain fresh and infectious, especially when we are sharing His truth with others.

The world-changer

The Jesus we follow is not an easy, comfortable option. When we were transformed by what He had done for us, our lives were separately turned upside down, inside out and back to front – to the point at which some of our friends struggled deeply with us in our home towns! It took us quite some time to work out how to follow Jesus and not be like some sort of inaccessible foreigner! However, although God has had a powerful impact on our lives, we still love many of the things we enjoyed before we were saved. It is a nightmare tearing Gavin away from the TV when the football is on, and Anne's head is often buried in the latest fashion magazine – some things will never change! Knowing Jesus and choosing to live for Him does not equal giving up who we are, following a set of rules, or living a staid life.

Following Jesus is life-changing. He is the greatest world-changer who ever lived. He is culture-changing, life-defining, and the least politically correct leader the world has ever known! He gave dignity to lepers, He empowered women when His culture saw them as an underclass, and He is radical and dangerous – walking through walls, turning over tables. He is not wishy-washy, comfortable, or commonplace! In those famous words, which have been prayed at many a church gathering, "My King is a King of knowledge. He's the wellspring of wisdom. He's the doorway of deliverance. He's the pathway of peace. He's the roadway of righteousness. He's the highway of holiness. He's the gateway of glory. He's the master of the mighty. He's the captain of the conquerors. He's the head of the heroes. He's the leader of the legislatures. He's the overseer of the overcomers. He's the governor of governors. He's the prince of princes. He's the King of kings and He's the Lord of lords. That's my King."[4] And this is just a tiny bit of what this preacher and pastor of Calvary Baptist Church (San Diego) said about Jesus! How easily we can lose a sense of who our God really is and what He has done.

Of course there is nothing wrong with raising our kids in the faith; in fact, if we know the Lord then we *must* raise them in His ways, and it's a real privilege for them. But are we giving them the full message? Following Jesus isn't easy. He might ask us to walk on water or we could go through incredible pain and suffering – living with Him is a roller-coaster ride. We don't want to follow a sanitized Jesus who is an over-familiar background figure. Somehow we need to get back to the wonder and not allow overexposure to all things "Christian" to stop people from encountering the true King of kings. The challenge is to present Jesus as "the way, the truth, and the life", affecting every area of our life in a powerful way, not someone we have become too familiar with or who doesn't make sense in the "real world". Anne hopes that one day her close friend can encounter the real truth about Jesus and truly know what he has been saved from.

Maybe you long for a fresh or first encounter with Jesus, or you feel a little too familiar with Him. Just imagine what life as a sheep without a shepherd would be like. If Psalm 23 was the testimony of a sheep without a shepherd, it might read like this...

The Lord is not my shepherd, I am so in need. I have nowhere to rest my weary head and am dead on my feet. There is no tranquillity in my life and no water to calm, nourish, and restore my soul. I have no guide in my life and no idea which path to choose; every step and decision is a lottery. As I walk through dark places I'm terrified, for I am entirely alone and enveloped by evil on all sides. There is no protection for me from any of it, no comfort at all to be found.

I am surrounded by my enemies and they are overpowering me. I have none of what I need to survive let alone thrive in this life. I know not of goodness and there seems to be no love around or within me. My days ahead will pass with great monotony and there is nothing for me beyond this life.

We thank the Lord that we have been found, that our testimony is instead that of a sheep *with* a Shepherd – the most amazing guide of all.

To think about...

- Does Christianity feel over-familiar to you? Maybe some lines are getting blurred and your salvation is a distant memory.

- Perhaps deep down you wish you had rebelled a bit – to see what all the fuss was about. That's OK, it's an honest feeling. However, maybe Jesus wants to remind you how proud and pleased He is to call you His child.

- Do you long for a fresh encounter with the risen Jesus? Why not ask Him now to remind you of what you have been saved from?

- Don't give up just because it all seems so familiar. Ask Jesus to show you a different aspect of who He is.

CHAPTER 9

Stumbling block:
Where are all the men?

(GAVIN AND ANNE)

"Christianity's primary delivery system, the local church, is perfectly designed to reach women and older folks. That's why our pews are filled with them. But this church system offers little to stir the masculine heart, so men find it dull and irrelevant. The more masculine the man, the more likely he is to dislike church."

David Murrow[1]

When I was growing up in London no one seemed to support the same football team as me. They all thought it was boring for a young man to support Wimbledon. Time has shown that they couldn't have been more wrong. In fact, what a journey all AFC Wimbledon fans have been on.

It was nine years since the English Football Association had allowed Wimbledon FC to be franchised off to Milton Keynes and the same FA had declared it "not in the wider interests of football" for a new club to be formed. Yet here we were at a massive stadium in Manchester with thousands of others supporting the re-formed AFC Wimbledon for this play-off final. The prize for the winners was a return to the

Football League. All that stood between us and that glittering reward was the opponents dressed in the gaudy orange of Luton Town.

The game was full of tension and I did my heart no good that day, as it felt as if I kicked every ball myself. Luton crashed a header against the post at the end of normal time, we missed a good chance in extra time, and then with twenty seconds left we fluffed a sitter with a missed header at the far post with the goal gaping. This all contrived to create the need for a penalty shoot-out to decide who was going up. I clung to hope and believed we could make it as I stood among thousands of fellow Wimbledon fans, all clad in our renowned yellow and blue. This was my tribe, my people, my culture; the London boys driven on by the injustice of having our Football League place stolen nine years earlier. Letting different guys take turns to start the singing, the stadium rocked to the sound of the passionate.

Wimbledon were doing well in the penalty shoot-out and soon enough we were one penalty away from winning the game and getting promoted. My heart was beating so fast I thought it might jump out of my chest entirely. Up stepped Mr Reliable, the club captain. In what seemed an eternity he walked forward and smashed the ball into the corner of the net. In an incredible moment of joy the cloud of tension evaporated at once and we danced and sang with all our might. The team and management were doing a jig on the pitch and we were copying them in the stands. The dejected Luton team and fans left quickly and the place was ours as we all strained our vocal cords and savoured the moment of corporate joy. What a game, what a day, what an effort, what a team!

Less than twenty-four hours later, I found myself in church. Here I encountered an altogether different experience. This felt nothing like my tribe. They were singing, but the whole thing was half-hearted and sombre, and no one seemed that happy to be there. There was a slight sense of the collective but people didn't seem as united as they had the day before. This was certainly not a culture that I felt entirely part of.

It struck me that men don't mind singing at football but struggle in church. My view is that singing at footie is active, as you can start the singing and choose which of the regular songs to belt out, with the throng joining in with you, while at church someone gets up and tells you which love songs to sing to Jesus. There are many similarities: the act of singing itself, the fact that there is a familiar collection of songs, the reality that it is all sung collectively. However, one is clearly active and the other passive. At the football I can start the singing and lead others, while at church I am a passive bystander who can join in if I feel the inclination to follow the invitation of a worship leader.

This doesn't just apply to singing, either. Church needs to be more active for men. If you want help clearing some wasteland to build a children's play park then there is no shortage of male volunteers. But to go and sit in a cold building singing love songs to Jesus that are picked by someone else, and then listen to a self-appointed expert talk for ages without right of reply, well, that's a different story...

Do the "math"!

My twenties were a really challenging time to be a Christian. I knew this stuff was real and I was never going to turn my back on it. I was amazed by all Jesus had done in my life, and had a great relationship with Him. The thing that made it so hard was how lonely it was. There were so few men anything like me in the church. I have always been a bit of a lad and never saw this as a barrier to Christianity until I found myself committed to church. I had no problem with others; it was just that there were so few guys who looked, sounded, and smelled like me!

I am for ever being asked by young lads why it is that you have to give up everything that's fun when you become a Christian. My answer is always the same: you don't. Before I met Jesus I loved footie, hanging out with my mates, and going for a beer. This remains the case today. I love the same things; it's just that I've met Jesus and this has given added meaning and value to my life that wasn't there before. We had a guy round for dinner once who was saying that he couldn't love God and Liverpool FC. My simple challenge to him was that, in fact, he could. As I pointed out, he didn't love Liverpool any more than I loved my beloved AFC Wimbledon. The difference was that now I had met Jesus I still loved my footie team loads, just nowhere near as much as I did the Saviour of the world!

The bottom line is that throughout my twenties (and indeed now into my thirties), the numbers simply haven't added up. Churches have been bereft of young men and I have often felt isolated. According to the Tearfund Report on church attendance in the UK across the full age ranges, the ratio of women (65 per cent) to men (35 per cent) is of real concern.[2] When you think that this is particularly pronounced in younger age groups, where the percentages are even more polarized, then we really do have cause for concern. The report also shows that the gap is widening and has been doing so for the last thirty years, so we must do something. Additionally, it is interesting that the report shows that other religions do not have the same problem. What is there in our theology that portrays church as girly? Perhaps we should look more seriously at whether we have over-feminized the gospel and the church.

It is a very worrying picture for the future. Without men in the church, we don't have future Christian fathers. American research has shown that when a mother is following Jesus and not a father, the family follows her 17 per cent of the time. However, when a father becomes a Christian the family follows 93 per cent of the time.[3] Not having men in the church is a stumbling block to both the men already there and the ones that could start coming. They want to feel able to build relationships and find a place of belonging, which is very tough without guys who they naturally connect with. I want nothing less than the growth of male numbers and percentages in the church – even if at the expense of women. However, I do long for greater parity. We need women in the church too! I am passionately egalitarian and it is this position that drives me to want a greater gender balance in the church.

****

What church do you join?

Our next door neighbour, Becky, and I gave birth to our daughters within nine months of each other and so began a connection that quite quickly grew into a great friendship.

My daughter, Amelie, would climb up on the armchair by the front window and wait for Becky's car to pull into next door's drive. Then without hesitation she would shout, "Mummy, please can we play with Chloë today – she's home now, Mummy, she's home!" Part of me would think, "Oh, poor Bec; I bet she sometimes wishes she wasn't bugged by next door the minute she returns from work," and yet the other part knew she'd be hearing the same from her daughter.

Today was no different. Up shot Amelie onto the chair and while I was in the middle of changing my son Daniel's nappy, she yelled, "Mummy, Becky's home. Can I play with Chloë? Please, Mummy, pleeeaaasssee?" I decided to succumb. I quickly pulled Daniel's trousers on, went to open the front door, shouted hello, and invited them in for a cup of tea. Gone were the old niceties from the time we first started to chat, and in their place were simple shouts and familiar approaches.

I could tell Becky had something on her mind, but unlike me she was not the sort of person to offload quickly – she took time to work through it and decide what to say. Amelie and Chloë raced upstairs to put on their princess dresses and begin their fashion show while I put the kettle on to boil. Instead of taking a comfy seat and relaxing, Bec was pacing the living-room floor.

"Good day?" I enquired.

"Well, it's not great," came the reply from the next room.

"Oh," I said. "What's going on?"

"Well, it's not good news, Anne."

We sat down opposite each other, cradling hot cups of tea, and hoping for enough peace to talk and listen.

"Spill," I said.

Tears quickly began to fill Becky's eyes as she spoke. "Matt is leaving me, Anne. I don't understand it; we have a beautiful daughter together, a lovely home, and yet it's not enough for him; he's leaving."

What on earth do you say in response to that? I sat there stunned for a few seconds, put my cuppa somewhere safe up high, and moved over to sit on the arm of her chair.

"Oh, Becky, I am *so so* sorry. What on earth has happened?" I said as I put my arm round her shoulders.

"I just don't know, Anne, I just don't get it. Granted, things haven't been as good as they could be (if you know what I mean), but we talk, we share life together, and there isn't another woman, as far as I know. It just doesn't make sense."

It didn't make sense to me either. "There must be a reason, Becky; people don't just end relationships like this." A fresh wave of tears poured down her face and I shot up a silent arrow prayer: "Please, Lord, don't let the girls come running downstairs now!"

With a choked voice Becky said, "I think he has just decided that he doesn't love me any more."

What do you say when someone says that? There wasn't much I *could* say except encourage her and tell her that we would be there for her.

Over the next few weeks Gavin and I watched a family fall apart. We saw Matt, with his head lowered, pack up his car and head for his new flat. We observed him come back every few nights to see his daughter. We prayed hard for Becky and Chloë, especially at night, as Becky really struggled to sleep in the house. I sat there day after day, particularly on Saturday, so grateful for my husband and two children and yet torn to pieces inside when I reflected on my neighbour's situation.

I asked Becky to a couple of things at church, and she came with me. I didn't want to thrust God in her face but I knew that through my hardest times I had massively valued my faith. Bit by bit I began to ask myself some interesting questions relating to Becky's situation. As she showed an interest in Christianity and saw more of my Christian friends, I wondered what was going to happen next for her, and to be honest I am still wondering.

When I thought about it, I was asking the question "Do I really want Becky to meet Jesus?" and every time the answer was "Of course I do – He would help her through this pain in a way that no one else could." But – and there was definitely a "but" – I was worried about the lack of men. Did I really want to introduce Becky to a world where there are very few men? You may laugh, but it really troubled me. Of course I wanted

Becky to have a relationship with God – that's the best thing she could ever have – but what would it mean for her future? Would she ever have another relationship with a man? Now of course I had gone too far in my thinking and it was (obviously) best just to take one day at a time and concentrate on loving my friend through a very difficult period in her life. However, because of the person I am, it did raise a series of questions in my mind.

Sadly not an isolated case

When I thought about the churches I had been in and the Christians I knew, I became increasingly aware that there was a distinct lack of decent fellas following God. When I thought about my best friend, Charlotte, I understood afresh why she didn't end up with a Christian guy. Growing up together, we went on a few Scripture Union holidays and on those camps we definitely had an experience of God. My best mate believed in God and prayed regularly, despite returning to a family who did not believe what she did. It was very hard for Charlotte to follow God as life moved on. There was pressure from home to "rethink" the crazy idea that there was a God, and there were attractive, capable men at university who had the potential to make a great life partner.

Whereas I managed to find one of the few strong Christian men at a fairly young age, Charlotte gave up and ended up choosing a man who had no faith at all. Now, don't get me wrong, he is an amazing guy and I love him a lot, but it has been extremely tough for Charlotte to keep a relationship with God going when her partner doesn't believe. She still believes in God, but that's where it ends.

Not meeting a Christian guy is a potential stumbling block to becoming a Christian and moving on in a relationship with

God. It sounds silly, but we are all human and we all want to be loved and to give love, so the idea that we might have to be alone through life is a very tough thing to face. There are some incredible women who have chosen to stay single, who even feel called to be single, but often the reason that they are single is the lack of suitable men in the church. And that grieves me deeply. Don't hear me wrong: I do believe that we can be with a non-Christian and keep our faith, and still find a way to serve God, but I am not convinced that it's God's best for us.

The problem is that our society tells us that we can have it all. We can buy the ingredients of a partner and kids; we can mix them together by buying or renting a property; we can bake the cake, leave it to cool, and ice it – all we need are nurseries, nannies, and two incomes – and off we go! So if we can find a way to do that, to have it all, you can guarantee that we will. After all, it's our right in the West to have all those things, isn't it… Couple that with the lack of men in the church, and what do we get? Well, we still gather all our ingredients. Perhaps a non-Christian man won't bring out quite the taste we wanted, but he will do because God obviously wants us to have it all.

And that's my struggle. If and when Becky meets God, would she ever go against society's pull and choose a life of singleness for the sake of her faith? I rarely see that happen.

The dream

I long for there to be more men in the church, and that there might be many different types of men who enter a relationship with Jesus that is not wishy-washy or lovey-dovey, because they can see that there is more to God than that. He threw stars into space, He created the world, He turned over the tax collectors' tables. He is accessible to all. Church can be guilty of painting a picture of a God who is so fluffy that many men would be embarrassed or cringe at the idea of being associated with Him. That guts me. My Gav is one of the strongest men I know, and he understands that God is all-powerful and able to confront people, and yet he is still able to enjoy life to the full. His relationship with God doesn't stop him playing or watching sport, it doesn't stop him having a laugh, and it doesn't demand that he has to suddenly become a wimp or hug and kiss his mates. Gav's faith is real and life-changing – I wish there were more like him.

Paul talks about singles and says that it is "good for them to stay unmarried, as I am" (1 Corinthians 7:8). I suppose that when we think about what he was called to do for Jesus, he was better off single (though some scholars believe he was in fact once married!). If he had been married, his poor wife would never have seen him and their relationship would have been virtually non-existent. He would have had to cut back on some of those missionary journeys so he could spend some evenings with his wife. And if they had had kids, that would have brought another challenge into play. Would he have needed to be around for childcare, would he have needed to give space for his wife to follow her call, or would their lives have revolved around him? Marriage throws up a whole host of questions that for Paul, it seems, were not an issue. Jesus called him and he did what he believed was right. Some women are in that situation too, and we could argue that they are truly "better off single".

There was a guy who really encouraged us earlier this year. He is a builder and a youth worker, and he came to our house to do some work for us. It was so exciting to see his passion for God and hear how difficult it has been for him to work on a building site as a Christian. (There are clearly very few guys in the trade who would associate themselves with God.) Anyway, he has decided to work with lads, giving them the chance to learn the building trade but also helping them grow in a relationship with Jesus. To him it doesn't seem like a big deal – he is just doing his bit for God – but we think it is incredibly important for the future of the church. We need more men like him.

Reflecting on the women's Alpha that we run at church, there is a real cause for concern. It is obviously important to share the gospel with anyone and everyone – that is what we are called to do – but it worries us that these new Christians return to their non-Christian men at home. They suddenly find themselves in a very difficult situation because their world view has changed and their lifestyle is often different. How do they make their relationships work? What do they do? After all, we don't want there to be an increase in family breakdown because of sharing the gospel. Is it realistic for us to expect their faith to keep on growing, or, if their partners are not interested, does it have to be kept "behind the scenes"?

We long for a way to change the tide and see a future of men like those first disciples, whom women can stand alongside. We need to see both genders standing together in equality of value and function and in equal numbers. We also pray that something can happen for women in these situations right now: that over the next few years we might see men coming back to Christ, meeting with Christ, and growing in Him.

What, as the people of God, can we do to draw in the men? Men's Alpha, building apprenticeships, role modelling from older men, street work, a setting to bring them into that doesn't scare them stupid... We don't have all the answers, but we do know that Jesus had twelve male disciples and they left their nets, their lives, to follow Him, so there is definitely somebody and something life-changing and worth following.

We want to pray and see an amazing revival among men

(and indeed all people) in Britain. But we dream of a new calibre of men who will stick by their partners, be committed Christians, be dads that hang around, and be men of integrity in their vocations, and men of passion in life. We recently received the following tweet and we don't just want it for our son but for everyone else's too:

> I want my son to be a better man than me. I want my daughter to marry a better man than me. But I wanna be a tough act to follow!

To think about...

- How many men do you know who are committed to Christ? Do you long for more? Is there anything we can do as the church to draw more men to Him?

- Are you finding waiting for a Christian man too difficult and if a non-believer came along would you give it a go? Do you really want to compromise? This is your whole life.

- Jesus was rugged and uncompromising. We need to recapture something of His character that often gets lost in our churches; to untame what it might mean to be a male follower of Jesus.

CHAPTER 10

Stumbling block:
I just don't have time!

(GAVIN AND ANNE)

> **"Time is more valuable than money.
> You can get more money but you cannot
> get more time."**

Jim Rohn

Youthful priorities

We love Wednesdays. Our house is filled with a bunch of young people who come to chat, hang out, eat rubbish, and talk about God stuff. They spill in through the door making a noisy hubbub while we pray that the kids will sleep through the mayhem. Our house is suddenly transformed from a quiet family sanctuary into an exciting, multi-scented, opinion-filled maelstrom that is bursting at the seams. We love it! Each one of them brings something unique and fun to the group and we always look forward to hearing what they have to say.

Near the beginning of last year we had been looking at different books of the Bible and trying to challenge one another to read more of it in our spare time and then discuss it. As we neared Lent we were continuing in the same vein of challenging and pushing each other to go deeper into God and want more of Him. I suppose we are not in the habit of gathering simply to entertain; we always want to bring something positive and meaningful out of any time we have with others. That must be why we wind people up sometimes, because we are never able to let them procrastinate – we constantly want to push others to reach their potential and do things that are out of their comfort zone. We only hope that we expect the same of ourselves as we do of others!

As we chatted with the young people about Lent, we decided that we should all give something up over the forty-day period. We wanted to do it not just to make ourselves feel better or perhaps to be healthier, but in order to get closer to Jesus. We had a common feeling that if we sacrificed something that was filling our time, we would have more available to spend with Jesus. We also wanted to honour Him more by quitting things that were not "good" for us because we were doing them too much.

We were amazed by the response. As we prayed and asked God to reveal to us what He wanted us to lay aside, every single person in the room knew what they should do. Bravely each one shared: give up smoking, stop using Facebook, quit eating rubbish, cease playing computer games, give up drinking alcohol, stop reading the wrong things. The list went on. God was clearly showing us what was filling our time and stopping us from finding space for Him. As we chatted about the hours some of this stuff was taking up, we were staggered by how long we spent on Facebook each week or just texting or playing computer games. We couldn't get over how often we were eating trash and how much some were spending on drinking and smoking.

Together we decided to change the way we were spending that time and instead give it to God. So the girl who was reading loads of unhelpful stuff stopped reading that and tried to start reading the Bible instead; the lad who was on his computer for most of his spare time attempted to stop it for forty days, and chose to use that time to try to seek God and get to know Him better. It was incredible. It was so challenging choosing to put God ahead of our daily wants and plans. It was surprising to see just how addictive so many things had become – even those things that we didn't associate with being addictive definitely could be. We supported each other in prayer and for those of us who could still go online, we wrote encouraging comments on our Facebook page.

Now it is fair to say that some of the group did not succeed in giving up their thing for the whole of Lent, but many did, and even those who didn't still felt challenged about how they were spending their time. What shocked us most of all was how much time we found to have a quiet time or do something else productive because our time wasn't being consumed by our habit. The most amazing thing was that many of us grew in our relationship with God – by that I mean we knew that we loved Him and that He loved us and that He was hungry for our time and attention, and that He could do more in us and through us when we were spending time in His presence. Obvious, you might think, but when we put it into practice over forty days we were massively shocked by the effect that it had on our lives.

It was also surprising to note how much we experienced spiritual attack. It took us a little while to realize what was happening, but we felt constantly tempted to pick up what we had given up, as if prompted "Once won't hurt". And we felt heavy at times and life threw up difficulties that made us want to return to our habit to reward ourselves with a nice time or feeling. The lesson we learned was that when we turned to God instead of to the thing we had given up, we were strengthened and encouraged much more than we would have been by the "quick fix" that the devil wanted us to pick up.

Looking back on that time now, we sometimes wish we still had the challenge of Lent to make us keep going in the same vein. Or maybe there is a way of finding some middle ground. The problem is that we humans are so weak that we quickly return to our old ways and find it very difficult to keep giving time over to God. Choosing, as Christians, to put God ahead of everything else that comes at us, in a sense to "give Him our first fruits", is very tough to maintain. How often have we heard in our own head the words "I just don't have time!"?

And yet God, down in the depths of our being, reminds us, "Yes, you do – I've already shown you; you do."

Time squeeze

The challenge facing so many Christians who have chosen to follow God and live for Him is finding time for Him. If we ourselves know how hard it is to build a relationship with God because of the constant busyness of life and the attractions of the world, how then do we help someone who doesn't know God at all to find time to enter into this relationship? It's very tough. These days we all seem so time-pressured. As the second line of the famous poem "The Paradox of our Age" by the fourteenth Dalai Lama says simply, we have "more conveniences, but less time".

Never before has life been so convenient, yet never has it been so pressurized. We work longer hours in Britain than ever before, waste hours commuting, and are constantly under strain. Modern society demands that women must pursue career and family, and men must be active dads and still climb the career ladder. All of this can be brilliant, but it does take up lots of time and energy. This time pressure even kicks in during schooldays, with the taxing exam league tables introduced in Britain placing immense and unnecessary strain on teenagers, their teachers, and their families. Everywhere we look, the whole world seems to have got itself into a big rush.

Take the advent of email as an example. What an incredible innovation it is. However, when "snail mail" was the norm we would not get a response to a letter for at least a few days. Contrast this with email, to which we can get a response almost instantly. Whereas an exchange of letters would take a few weeks, the same amount of correspondence via email now takes a matter of hours. This has got even more pronounced in recent times with technological advances. Just a few years ago we could only email on a computer, but now our mobile phone allows us never to be out of reach of our email, phone messages, and Twitter and Facebook accounts. It can all get a bit much.

If we think about one of our closest friends, who works full-time, plays sport three times a week, lives with her partner, cooks most evenings, cleans her house, shops, and spends a bit of time with friends and online – how does she find space to meet with Jesus and get to know Him? Where would He fit in? Or those young people whom we saw decide to follow Jesus in a cattle shed last summer: how do they begin to build that relationship when they go home? What do they have to change? Anything? And who helps them figure that out anyway? You can hear that phrase already tripping off their tongue, and our friend's: "I just don't have time!"

Is all this really true? Are we genuinely living in such time poverty that we can't make space for Jesus? American wellness coach Diane Randall says that "lack of time is more perception than reality. The problem is the lack of commitment to your priorities after you've set them. People overwork, set time to watch television and surf the Internet, but many people don't set time to do the things that they say are important to them."[1] And here lies the problem. We don't have less time than previous generations; we just choose to spend it differently. If Jesus is a priority in our lives then we will make time for Him.

If we treated some of our earthly relationships the way we often treat God, then would those relationships last, or would they more likely wither away due to lack of investment? We would never treat our partner the way we so often treat Jesus. We would never give our closest friends only the "fag end" of our time. We wouldn't dream of only ever allowing our children to have our attention on our terms, when we can be bothered and when nothing more enticing is on offer. Just because God is always there for us does not mean we should abuse His grace. If nothing else, it is unbelievably disrespectful towards the King of kings.

Indulge us for a moment and imagine that God Himself in fact treated us as we so often treat Him, and didn't make time for us. Though it's a little twee, we find the following anonymous poem profoundly challenging with regard to the idea that we have no time for God and as such He reciprocates that mentality towards us...

I knelt to pray but not for long.
I had too much to do.
I had to hurry and get to work
for bills would soon be due.
So I knelt and said a hurried prayer
and jumped up off my knees.
My Christian duty was now done.
My soul could rest at ease.
Now all day long I had no time
to spread a word of cheer.
No time to speak of Christ to friends.
They'd laugh at me I'd fear.
"No time. No time. Too much to do,"

That was my constant cry.
No time to give to souls in need.
At last the time to die.
I went before the Lord, I came,
I stood with downcast eyes.
For in his hands God held a book;
It was the book of life.
God looked into his book and said,
"Your name I cannot find.
I once was going to write it down
but never found the time."[2]

(Source: www.turnbacktogod.com)

We are so profoundly grateful that the God for whom we are so often guilty of not finding enough time has grace that is sufficient for our iniquities. We are so thankful that Jesus doesn't treat us anything like as badly as we so often treat Him. We can claim to have no time for God, but it's simply not true. We have time for friends, family, work, chores, sport, television, social networking. Embarrassingly, the list of things we have time for is endless. Therefore we clearly have time for Jesus. It's just a matter of *choosing* to spend time with Him.

New focus

The Bible passage that has really challenged us over this is the story of the sisters Mary and Martha, found in Luke 10. Martha is running around preparing her house and a meal for Jesus – which you naturally would be doing if Jesus was coming to visit! (After all, He is the Creator of the world. Just imagine how you would behave if an important visitor such as the UK prime minister or US president were popping in for a visit.)

Conversely, Mary does not rush around at all. She sits at the Lord's feet listening to Him and spending quality time in His presence, not slaving away on His behalf when He hasn't even asked her to, as her sister does.

The different approaches of the sisters clearly lead to tension. Martha is obviously very frustrated with Mary and complains to Jesus that she is not helping her. Why is Mary not pulling her weight? From a human point of view we expect Jesus to encourage Mary to help her sister, but He doesn't. Fair enough, she isn't watching TV, but surely getting the meal ready would be more helpful? But Jesus says, "Mary has chosen what is better" (verse 42). I think if He said that to me I would still want to argue, as Martha would, "But I need help here right now!" However, what challenges me in Jesus' words is what He says just before that line: "Martha, Martha, you are worried and upset about many things, but only one thing is needed" (verses 41–42) – basically Jesus is the thing she needs.

Now we don't for a minute think that this means we shouldn't cook a meal or prepare the house for the arrival of guests, but what is interesting is the challenge over the way that Martha is doing it. You can almost hear that little phrase in her mind: "I just don't have enough time!" And the result of that stress is that she is worrying and feeling upset about many things. She is a practical person and is putting pressure on herself to make an excellent dinner instead of realizing that time with Jesus is more important.

Jesus addresses Martha's mindset. He wants her to stop and know that He is her God as much as He is Mary's. He wants her to realize that He is more important than anything else she is doing. Not to big Him up, but so that she can receive His peace, His strength, and the knowledge of His love in such a way that the worry and upset are less and her focus is different. Jesus doesn't ask us to stop doing the things we are meant to do;

He challenges us to prioritize them and include Him in them. Noble acts are important, but this encounter clearly shows that nothing should take precedence over spending time with God. The theologian Michael Wilcock puts it this way in his appraisal of Mary's actions over those of the bustling Martha:

> When Jesus expects us to follow him all the way, he means not a frenzy of religious activity undertaken in our own strength, but the total abandonment of ourselves to him, for him to work in us both to will and to work for his good pleasure. [3]

God wants our time

We can be in danger of putting God into a little box labelled "quiet time" and then not allowing Him into the rest of our day. He doesn't want this. He's eager for our time and desperate for us to share our lives with Him. We come across so many parents of teenagers who want nothing more than for their children to engage with them, to share some of their lives with them, instead of being embarrassed by them, ignoring their existence, and grunting any scrap of conversation their way. God is no different; He craves our time.

He wants an individual relationship with us and not just a group one. It's easy to pray in groups or at church, but He wants a relationship with us in the quiet spaces too, when no one is looking. He wants us to go deeper with Him. He wants to be part of our everyday life. For Gav, when he first came to faith he was playing football in goal a few times a week. This meant standing at one end of the pitch on his own for a lot of the game. Gav would say that in those moments he had some incredible encounters with God and also some everyday chit-chat. God wants to be part of the everyday. Not just in church or on solemn occasions; He wants to be involved in all of our life.

It was often said of that great heroine of the faith Corrie ten Boom, who survived being sent to a Nazi concentration camp as punishment for hiding Jews during World War Two, that you were never sure when she was talking to you or when she was praying. So natural was her relationship with Jesus that it slipped into the conversation all over the place. We long for a relationship that close, in which the Lord is not a bystander in our life but is directly involved in it all. We want to engage with God as naturally as we would with any person standing in front of us.

Jesus knows the importance of spending time with His Father. He had such a natural way of corresponding with His Father in heaven while He was on earth. We read in Matthew 14:22: "Immediately Jesus made the disciples ... go on ahead of him to the other side, while he dismissed the crowd. After he had dismissed them, he went up on a mountainside by himself to pray." Jesus also called on His Father right in the middle of what He was doing: "And he directed the people to sit down on the grass. Taking the five loaves and the two fish and looking up to heaven, he gave thanks and broke the loaves. Then he gave them to the disciples, and the disciples gave them to the people" (Matthew 14:19).

Jesus involved His Father in His daily life but He also made space to be with Him on His own. We too must make space and time for God. We cannot allow ourselves to be too busy to spend time with the Almighty. We will never forget an OHP slide (wow, that's retro!) shown while we were studying at Bible college. It had a picture of a man at a desk with a massively full in tray and an empty out tray. The man was working unbelievably hard yet getting nowhere. At the edge of his desk and out of his line of sight were a few phone messages that he was far from getting round to. They said things such as, "God rang to speak to you. He would like you to ring back", and "God phoned. He misses your chats and would love you to get in touch." Most profound of all was the unread message on the top of the pile: "God called just to talk."

To think about...

- Are you ready to listen? God longs to talk to us.

- Is it really true that we don't have time? Is it about re-ordering our priorities?

- Perhaps it is Lent again, or any time of year and God is challenging you to make time for Him. Is there something you could give up and/or take up to show God that you mean business in your relationship with Him?

CHAPTER 11

Stumbling block:
Quick-fix Christianity

(GAVIN)

**Frodo: "Go back, Sam. I'm going to Mordor alone."
Sam: "Of course you are. And I'm coming with you."**

Taken from *The Lord of the Rings: The Fellowship of the Ring*[1]

Many of my Sundays involve leaving Anne in bed at the crack of dawn and travelling to some far-flung corner of Britain to preach in a church. On one particular Sunday I had just finished preaching my heart out and was drinking what I considered to be a much-deserved cup of coffee and chomping on a custard cream while chatting to a friendly mum. A man in his late forties was shuffling towards me, looking rather nervous. I noticed him hovering a short distance away, shifting from foot to foot and perhaps wondering whether it was worth waiting to chat at all. When the lady I was with had got her answer and finished pouring out her heart about her teenage twins, the guy finally grabbed his moment to approach me. With head bowed and hands wringing together, he told me how he was struggling with his son. This is a scene so often repeated in my life. Christian parents of teenage kids are always concerned more than anything about the faith of their teens.

This guy's son was fourteen years old and they had previously enjoyed a strong relationship, but now all of a sudden he was finding him very difficult to communicate with. In short, their relationship had broken down. The dad was clearly distraught about the situation, his anguish visible in the beads of sweat that were dripping down from his brow as he spoke. He had quite clearly been very close to his son over the years, spending a good deal of time with him, and sharing a lot. But now, hitting a challenging age, his boy had become (to his mind) distant and interested in doing only things that his dad did not want to do. I enquired what these were, and it became clear that computer games were high on his teenage son's agenda, and he would spend hours holed away in his bedroom engrossed in that world, a million miles from anything his dad might be doing.

What was so encouraging about this encounter was how much that dad still cared! It was so refreshing to see and hear a father who loved his son so much that he longed for his time and attention, and wasn't just pleased that he was keeping himself busy and "out of his hair". I knew I had to try to help. I shot up an arrow prayer: "Lord, help me here and now. What should this guy do to get through to his son?" For a minute I felt a bit helpless. I don't have teenagers; my son is a pre-schooler who likes nothing more than playing with me and having my undivided attention. Granted, I used to be a teenager, and I lead Youth for Christ, but who was I to minister in this situation? I was tempted just to encourage him to talk to his lad and try to open up communication that way, but I knew that would seem like an easy answer. How unsubstantial and paltry an offering that would be.

This guy had come to me; it was clearly costly for him to do it, so there had to be something helpful I could suggest. I knew that I mustn't shoot from the hip too quickly, as I was often in the habit of doing, but there had to be a way for this man to find a formula for communicating better with his son.

"O Lord, what should I say?" Out of nowhere came a thought.

"When he was little, what did he like to play with?" I asked.

"Trains and Tonka trucks," came the reply.

"And did you leave him to play with them on his own, or did you get involved?" I queried.

"I got down on the floor and played with him, rolling the trucks up and down for hours!" he said, a nostalgic smile coming across his face.

"OK, so now he likes computer games, does he?"

"He does," came the instant response.

"Do you play them with him?" I questioned.

"Oh, no, he locks himself away and plays by himself or with friends... it's not really my thing," his dad added.

The whole conversation was intriguing me, so I pushed on with it. "Why, when he was little, did you get involved and play, but now you leave him to it?"

"I find it difficult to engage with," he concluded.

I wasn't going to give up on this one; why stop reaching out to your kids in their areas of interest just because a sweaty, hairy teenager has replaced a cute toddler? Computer games might have replaced Thomas the Tank Engine but the principles of meeting your children where they are at remain the same.

"How about stopping on your way home and buying a new computer game for his console?" I suggested.

The guy looked shocked. "Are you serious?" he said, looking increasingly bemused.

"Bear with me," I replied. "Not a gift to give him to take him away from you even more, but a game that you can play too. A game that you don't find too offensive but one that your son would like to play – one in the charts that he hasn't got – then take it home, give the game to him, and suggest that you have bought this for the two of you to play together. Don't let him play it on his own, because he will get too good and immediately outplay you! No, make it something that you do, just the two of you together. Your time, your space, your chance to get to know who and where he is right now."

Wow, brainwave: where did that come from? I looked thankfully heavenwards. The father looked thrilled by the idea, a quizzical "Why didn't I think of that?" expression passing over his face. Things are so obvious once they are pointed out to us. His son was still his boy, however old, and stylistic preferences on use of leisure time were not a big enough issue to come between them. As the dad walked away his head was held higher and he seemed much more positive. Now he was no longer a desperate man with no way forward; he was a man with a plan. Fair enough, it might not work, but he had hope, and instead of just watching the months roll by and the relationship worsen, he could try to find a way in.

Isn't God incredible? Sometimes the simplest, most obvious things are not the first ones we think to do or say, and yet once a suggestion is out there it makes so much sense! God is good. He so often works in simple yet profound ways, doesn't He?

Powerful outcomes

A year later I was speaking at the same church because they had kindly invited me back to minister again (it always helps to return to the same place to continue the journey with people!). After the service a lad of about fifteen came over to chat to me. I could tell he was about fifteen because he walked with a swagger, his jeans hanging low, and he had a rather bumpy complexion. Here was a guy who was trying to figure out his place in the world. As he shuffled over in his thick-laced trainers, I wondered what this conversation would involve. Was it about a relationship he was embarking on: had something in the talk spoken to him? Maybe God was challenging him. It is always exciting seeing and hearing about how Jesus is at work in young people. Anyway, as the lad began to talk it was not what I expected at all.

"I have come to say thank you, Gav," he uttered.

"No problem; it's great to be with you again," I responded.

"No, not thanks for today, but thanks for what you said to my dad a year ago."

(Oh, so he hasn't been listening to a word I said this morning – as a preacher these thoughts cannot help but race through your mind!) Racking my brains I quickly tried to remember what he was referring to. Thankfully the lad reminded me: "My dad started playing computer games with me about a year ago – you told him to buy one, and we have been playing them ever since. Thank you. We have a wicked relationship now."

Now I am not usually very emotional, but this simple statement at the end really tugged at my heart. How incredible is God? He gives you a simple thought and He uses it in such an obvious way, and yet it dramatically changes a relationship. What blew me away as well was that this father was committed to his son through tough times, and he wanted to stay close to him no matter what changes were happening in his life. Even though this dad faced a bunch of teenage hurdles, he was determined to find a way over them to his son. But what fascinated me even more was that this father had happily engaged with his son when he was small, but then when it got harder he could have just completely given up.

So often we involve ourselves in people's journeys only when it suits us. When we can connect and identify with where they are, we jump in and get involved, but when their situation or their choices change, we are tempted to jump ship. They can present us with stumbling blocks that make us want to give up on accompanying them. Some of us can lead people to Jesus because that is what we do and we are quite good at it, but what happens to them afterwards? Do we care if their walk continues? Often it can require us to do something uncomfortable – like playing computer games – and so we avoid it, potentially seriously damaging a relationship.

That dad didn't leave it too late, and he was reconciled with his son. As the classic Billy Ocean song says, when the going got tough in his son's life, he responded by getting going to reach out to his son.[2] When it's really challenging, those of character step up to the action, not out into oblivion. He did leave it for a while, but then he found a way through. When he really needed to step up he humbled himself and went out of his way to make things work with his son. In the same way that he had played with trucks and trains for his son's benefit, he now played computer games. Would he have chosen that? Certainly not! Did he have a choice in the end? No: the relationship was simply too important to let slide.

Loving others

If we are truly seeking to love God with all our heart, soul, mind, and strength, what does that mean in relation to loving others? It demands a level of sacrifice, of going out on a limb, of discomfort, to help others move on in God and to show them a greater understanding of the Father's love. Our pastor's wife said the other day that if we feel responsible for someone in any way then we should never let them stay where they are. Instead, we should always help them to make positive steps forward. That really made us reflect: how often are we overcoming the obstacles around others and encouraging them to face them and keep pushing into God? When it is easy, we get involved; when it demands our energy, our time or confrontation, or requires us to do anything that is uncomfortable or sacrificial, we put it off – or, worse, leave it altogether.

Jesus is amazing in this. His model to us of real love – of keeping involved, of investing no matter what, of putting in the hard hours, is powerful. To be good at anything requires a lot of time and effort. The writer Malcolm Gladwell claims that it takes 10,000 hours of practice ever to become an expert at anything.[3] When Anne was younger she used to play the flute, and did hours of practice that enabled her to keep improving and take the exams. If she picked up her flute again now she would probably have to start at the beginning and slowly remember how to play! The challenge for so many of us today is to get into the habit of sticking by people and not to stop practising, so that we might become experts at supporting others.

The Jesus model

Look at what Jesus did with the disciples: He shared life with them. When He said, "Come and follow Me" (Matthew 4:19), He stuck with them. He didn't walk away when they fell asleep in the garden (Matthew 26:40,43). He didn't give up when one of them betrayed Him (Matthew 26:23). He reinstated one when he denied Him (John 21:15). He kept encouraging them when they doubted Him (John 20:24–29). He kept responding when they asked crazy questions such as "Who is the greatest?" (Matthew 18:1) and He kept explaining when they didn't understand what His mission was. And that's just a brief look at Jesus' journey with the disciples. The reality was that Jesus was committed to them; He wasn't a one-hit wonder in their lives.

So often we witness a crazy turnover in the marketplace, with people in jobs for just a couple of years or less. We live in an instant culture where we get our "hit" and move on. How can this not affect our relationships? We can be guilty of finding immediate pleasure in something and then moving on to the next thing, or we might stick at it for a while but, when the going gets tough, we look elsewhere. Just observe the number of broken relationships. We are all about self-satisfaction and pleasure, not about putting others first. We are just as guilty of that ourselves.

There was a young person in our youth group who had been struggling with some problems and we knew that if we addressed them it would take a lot of time, and possibly pain and energy, to help that individual – so what did we do? We hoped someone else would sort it – prayed that someone would – and then watched, hoping that it wouldn't fall to us! How sinful, yet honest, is that! But then when Jesus got us by the scruff of the neck we knew it was ours to deal with: "If you really love Me, feed My sheep" (John 21:15–17) And the result? Much simpler than we could have imagined: a powerful example of God at work and a deeper understanding of His love for others. So why didn't we do it earlier?

Share the journey

Stickability is crucial in people's lives. It means not leaving people where they are; not allowing them to slip away from Jesus; not giving up but hanging in there and meaning business. Ultimately, it involves showing the real love of Christ, not just a tiny bit of Him. Some of us find it harder than others, because we have a limited understanding of love ourselves and therefore struggle to love more. This is not an excuse to avoid finding a way to love; it is an insight that highlights the need for all of us to ask God to show us how to love better – to know when to reach out and be more selfless, and to put others ahead of ourselves. We fear it is costly, and it is, but what does it mean for the rest of our lives?

So often we feel that we cannot be bothered because whatever we are "meant" to be doing does not fit in with our desired plan for the day or evening ahead. At those moments we have a choice: we can let our inner selves dictate what we will do, or we can choose to be selfless and do what we are meant to be doing. Which option is ultimately more fulfilling? If we were to ask that man from the church to talk to us about his relationship with his son now, he would be a different guy. No longer hanging his head and wringing his hands, but knowing a joy and a fulfilment that come only from sacrifice and sticking at something even when it is really challenging and demands exceptional selflessness.

What is amazing in all of this is that although we are decidedly human and weak and although we live in a society that is ever-changing and evolving, we all massively value the consistent relationships in our lives. The challenge facing us is to learn how to stick at things even when others don't, because then we show people a different way and we point to a greater love: a love that shocks people because they have never witnessed it before.

I was recently playing golf with a good friend of mine who is a youth worker, and I asked him what he thought was the biggest stumbling block to people making it in faith. Without a moment's hesitation he said that it was the fact that we don't share the journey with people. We give up on them when it's too hard. We consider a decision to follow Jesus to be a tick on some sort of register, and then move on to the next person. When are we going to realize that each life is important and worth sticking with and fighting for? After all, we believe in a

God who would never give up on us.

That phrase that is scattered throughout the Old Testament (Deuteronomy 31:6, 8; Joshua 1:5; 1 Kings 8:57) and referred to again in the New (Hebrews 13:5) – "I will never leave you nor forsake you" – represents an incredible reality. If this is the God we serve – a God who sticks with us, no matter what – are we modelling this to others, or are we allowing our own personal hurdles to cause us to stumble and stop us from committing for the long haul?

To think about...

- Have you bought into this instant culture that we find ourselves entrenched in?

- Are you prepared to stick with people for the long haul or do you give up at the first obstacle? If we are going to see lasting fruit in people's lives we have to keep journeying together.

- Who needs you right now? Let's think less "Me first" and more "Who is in need of a friend?"

Don't give up on God. He hasn't given up on you and never will.

Conclusion

(GAVIN AND ANNE)

"The greater the obstacle, the more glory
in overcoming it."

Molière (1622–73)

An unbelievable moment

Derek Redmond is one of the most inspiring athletes ever to
have graced our screens. Much favoured to gain a medal in the
400-metre sprint at the 1992 Barcelona Olympics, if not to win
outright, the British sprinter had the world at his feet. Those
of us who are old enough might remember the semi-final of
the qualifiers, in which he famously tore his hamstring while
running. But we don't remember him because he got injured;
we recall him because of his response to such adversity.
Redmond was passionate about winning that semi-final; he
was such an incredible athlete and had trained long and hard
for four years to get to that position. Yet suddenly a searing
pain ripped through his leg. He fell to the ground in agony,
but instead of staying down and ending his race there and
then, Derek chose to battle with the pain tearing through his
hamstring and limp his way over the remaining 250 metres to
the finish line.

It is a scene that has become one of the most enduring
and iconic in modern Olympic history. There was Redmond,
hopping along in pain, with people all over the world and the
thousands in the stadium looking on. Suddenly a man broke
through the security lines and ran over to help Derek finish the

race. This kind of action was not only illegal but unheard of in an Olympic arena. The guy put an arm around Redmond's shoulder and spoke encouragement into his ear to strengthen his resolve. As the two men neared the end of the race, he stood back to let Derek cross the line on his own. As he did so, over 65,000 people gave him the most incredible standing ovation. The sound was deafening; it was the greatest noise made in that stadium at any point in the Games. Even though Derek did not win the race, the reaction from the crowd was such as to crown him the winner. His dramatic fall yet anguished commitment to completing the race spoke volumes to those watching. I mean, does anyone remember who actually *won* that semi-final?

It emerged afterwards that the man who helped Redmond hobble towards the line was in fact his father: a father helping a son to keep going when he was at his lowest and weakest point; a father who never took his eyes off his son in the race and then, when he fell, went over and gave him the vital support he needed. He provided the most incredible shoulder for Derek to lean on in his most vulnerable and difficult moments. *The Guardian* newspaper put it like this: "What made this moment at the 1992 Games special was it brought into focus not just one athlete's near-heroic desperation but a more universal theme: the nature of parenthood."[1]

Redmond's race not only inspired the thousands watching in Barcelona and the millions around the world, it also massively touched his fellow competitors – who must have known he was favoured to win a medal in the final. Derek received many messages from the other runners, but this one, from a Canadian competitor he had never met, stands out:

Long after the names of the medalists have faded from our minds, you will be remembered for having finished, for having tried so hard, for having a father to demonstrate the strength of his love for his son. I thank you, and I will always remember your race and I will always remember you – the purest, most courageous example of grit and determination I have seen.[2]

Something incredible happened that day, not just in Derek but in every one of those watching. Why did the people give him a standing ovation? How amazing was it that he did not stumble to the ground in floods of tears and then hobble off to the side? Equally touching was the man who came to his aid – especially before we knew it was his father! But realizing it was his dad makes the whole story speak to us in a different way. There is something in us that knows that there is more glory in rising when we fall than in winning with ease. Inside each one of us lives the reality that it is better to keep going even when the circumstances are against us, and instinctively we know that it is right to give glory to those who triumph over agonizing adversity.

It is the fact that his dad came to Derek's aid that touches our hearts as well. He was not left to suffer alone – of all people, his dad came to lift him up both emotionally and physically, and encourage him. Yes, Derek had already made the decision to keep going, but his dad's support will not only have made those steps easier but will have provided a strength that he desperately needed at that moment. There is a great clip on YouTube of that 400-metre race, with the song "You raise me up"[3] playing behind, and it's awesome to hear the line about finding strength on another's shoulders as you watch a father just being that shoulder.[4]

What about us?

Yes, we have inner resolve, and, yes, we can keep going through some things, but involving God – our heavenly Father – in the race of life is surely the best way. We cannot keep going through pain, through challenges, through being let down, through our own weaknesses and disappointments, through illness, through lack of feelings or people trying to steal our faith, without a personal assurance that God literally comes to our aid in all these things. There is no point knowing that He is sitting in the crowd watching us when we face hard times that can cripple us to the point of giving up. We need Him right by our side in the midst of it, so that no matter what hits us, no matter how we feel, we keep going and cross the line.

Derek did not let the others in the race decide his future, he didn't let the reaction of the crowd determine his decision, and he knew he wanted to get over that line – however odd it looked. The challenge is: are we affected so much by those around us that the stumbling blocks have become too difficult to overcome? Or are we so damaged by stuff that has happened to us that we have limped to the side and lost sight of the finishing line? Some of us don't even know that there is a Father who will come to our aid if we ask Him, but the truth is, He is waiting. He says, "I stand at the door and knock. If anyone hears my voice and opens the door, I will come in and eat with him, and he with me" (Revelation 3:20). He doesn't say He will force His way in – we have to choose to open the door – but, if we do, He promises to come in. And then, no matter how we feel or what life brings, He doesn't, at any point, walk out on us.

There were times as we walked through the journey of having baby Daniel when we felt like Derek – in that moment of agony, when he knew it would be far from a smooth finish. But we still had a choice of what to do. There have been times when we have all known Christians whom we respected and trusted do crazy things or let us down beyond what we thought possible. Many of us have experienced Christ's power, but have also known times when such feelings are a million miles away – and yet we still choose how to respond. Life has often dealt us a hand of cards that we don't want to play, and don't know *how* to play, especially when we have prayed and prayed and waited and waited for something in particular to change. Church has let us down many times: people have not been what we expected them to be, we have lived with disappointment, and it has brought us low. Yet we still have a choice of what to do.

We can go and sit on the sidelines and be spectators, never really getting involved in the action. We can battle on alone and keep looking for answers in other people and in what the world presents us with. We could collapse in a heap and hope that one day we will have the strength to get up. Or we could find a way to overcome the hurdles in front of us. The only way we know of doing that is with Christ: the only one who doesn't let us down; the only one who will come back at the end of time and whose kingdom will come and whose will will be done on earth and in heaven.

If we let Him, He will lay a foundation of strength and determination in our hearts and lives. He will give us bedrock that we can trust in and through everything. We just have to invite Him. And no matter what we have done or how long we have sat in a heap on the sidelines or tried to run a different way, He still invites us to dust ourselves down and finish the race with Him, and know a fullness of life that we have never experienced before.

We long that, like Derek with his father's help, you would invite Christ to take up that position in your life so that He becomes more important than anything else. We have found that having Jesus in our individual lives shines a light on the dark blocks that cause us to stumble, and that light continues to guide us over some and through others. And no matter how big the boulders appear to be or how dark they get, the light is always greater than the blackness that surrounds them.

And the truth is that if you finish the race with Christ, His glory will be seen in a way that it never would have been otherwise, because you have overcome and held on to Him. The standing ovation will ultimately go to Him.

This is what we are living for: to keep racing with Christ and ultimately make Him stand. Don't let the stumbling blocks define your journey of faith. Let the Saviour of the world do so instead. It never promises to be easy, but following Jesus is the most amazing thing we can ever do. Jesus says to us right now what He said to His first disciples: "Come, follow Me."

Are you in?

Maybe you want to pray...

God of many names, my name is known to you.
I am held in the hand of your life, and I do not know what you will make of me.
All I know is that I cannot make myself any more than I could in my mother's womb.
But this I can do, this I choose.
To give myself into the hand of your continuing creativity;
my past, with its joys and triumphs, its failures and regrets;
my present, with its struggles and accomplishments, its hopes and setbacks;
my future, with its fears and freedom, its pain and promise.
To loose and to bind, to stretch and to shape, to become what I will,
trusting the hand that made the world
trusting the spirit that breathes life
trusting the love that will not let me go
trusting the promise of the Word made flesh.
Amen.[5]

Notes

Chapter 1: Stumbling block: *Fallen idols*
1. M. Eaton, *Preaching through the Bible: 2 Samuel* (Tonbridge: Sovereign World, 1996), p. 68.

Chapter 2: Stumbling block: *Faith stealers*
1. From chapter 2 of *The Picture of Dorian Gray* (1890).
2. Article entitled "Six Reasons Young Christians Leave Church", 28 September 2011 (www.barna.org).

Chapter 3: Stumbling block: *I feel sceptical and cynical*
1. Research originally from LifeWay Research and quoted in an article on www.usatoday.com entitled "Survey: non-attendees find faith outside Church", www.usatoday.com/news/.../2008-01-09-unchurched-survey_N.htm
2. Article on www.ligonier.org by R. C. Sproul entitled "Is the Church full of hypocrites?"

Chapter 4: Stumbling block: *When the feelings go*
1. Directed by George Lucas, 2002.
2. F. Darabont, *The Shawshank Redemption* (New York: Newmarket Press, 1996).
3. *The Independent* newspaper, 30 March 2011: article entitled "Marriage rates fall to record low".

Chapter 5: Stumbling block: *I hate church*
1. *Time* Magazine, Friday 31 May, 1963.
2. L. Sweet, *Postmodern Pilgrims: A 1st Century Passion for a 21st Century Church* (Broadman & Holman Publishers, 2000).
3. Such as "The Quest for Community" on www.leonardsweet.com

Chapter 6: Stumbling block: *Broken dreams*
1. *The Guardian* newspaper, 17 April 2010, article entitled "I want to be famous".
2. When I grow up I want to be... study, www.taylorherring.com/blog/index.php/tag/traditional-careers

Chapter 7: Stumbling block: *When life is bad*
1. By J. K. Rowling (Bloomsbury Publishers, 1999).
2. Matt Redman, "You never let go", from the album *Beautiful News* (Kingsway Music, 2007).

Chapter 8: Stumbling block: *Christianity feels mundane*

1. Henri J. M. Nouwen, *The Return of the Prodigal Son* (Darton, Longman & Todd, 1992), p. 70.

2. Henri J. M. Nouwen, *The Return of the Prodigal Son* (Darton, Longman & Todd, 1992), pp. 74–5.

3. R. Parsons, *Getting Your Kids Through Church Without Them Ending Up Hating God* (Oxford: Monarch Books, 2011), p. 91.

4. "That's my King", by Dr S. M. Lockridge (sermon in Detroit, 1976).

Chapter 9: Stumbling block: *Where are all the men?*

1. D. Murrow, *Why do men hate going to church?* www.churchformen.com

2. *Report on Churchgoing in the UK* (Tearfund, 2007).

3. B. Peel, *What God Does When Men Lead: The Power and Potential of Regular Guys* (Tyndale House Publishers, 2010).

Chapter 10: Stumbling block: *I just don't have time!*

1. D. Randall, article entitled "Lack of time! Perception or reality" on www.witi.com

2. Georgy N Joseph, poem source: www.turnbacktogod.com/no-time-for-god

3. M. Wilcock, *The Saviour of the World: The Message of Luke's Gospel* (Downers Grove: InterVarsity Press, 1979), p. 124.

Chapter 11: Stumbling block: *Quick-fix Christianity*

1. Directed by Peter Jackson, 2001.

2. "When the going gets tough, the tough get going", written by Wayne Braithwaite, Willy Head, Barry Eastmond, Robert John "Mutt" Lange and Billy Ocean, 1985.

3. M. Gladwell, *Outliers: The Story of Success* (Little, Brown & Company, 2008).

Conclusion

1. *The Guardian* newspaper article history, Simon Burnton (re post 30/11/06).

2. *The Guardian* newspaper article history, Simon Burnton (re post 30/11/06).

3. A song written in 2002 with music by Secret Garden's Rolf Løvland and lyrics by Brendan Graham.

4. YouTube.com, uploaded by necessity4failure.com: "Powerful inspirational story... Don't give up."

5. www.freshworship.org: dedication by Kathy Galloway from the book *Talking to the Bones* (SPCK, 1996).